AMERICA'S REGIONAL COOKBOOK

AMERICA'S REGIONAL COOKBOOK

BETTY EVANS

Gulf Publishing Company
Houston, Texas

*For Gordon
and our three children,
Bob, Suzanne, and Jeanne,
with special thanks for their love and
support of my cookbook adventures.*

America's Regional Cookbook

Copyright © 1997 by Betty Evans. All rights reserved. This book, or parts thereof, may not be reproduced in any form without permission of the publisher and the author.

Gulf Publishing Company
Book Division
P. O. Box 2608 ☐ Houston, Texas 77252-2608

10 9 8 7 6 5 4 3 2 1

Library of Congress Cataloging-in-Publication Data
  Evans, Betty.
    America's regional cookbook / Betty Evans.
      p. cm.
    Includes index.
    ISBN 0-88415-105-0
    1. Cookery, American.   I. Title.
  TX715.E8812   1996
    641.5973—dc20   96-26966
                                                              CIP
Illustrations on pages xii, 26, 50, 78, 100, 118, 136, and 168 by Senta Eva Rivera.

CONTENTS

Acknowledgments, xiii

Foreword, xv

Preface, xvii

New England   1

Paula's Mystic Hot Crab Dip, 3 • Corn Chowder, 3 • Boston Clam Chowder, 4 • East Coast Steamed Lobster, 5 • Don's Oyster Stew, 6 • Cape Cod Clam Pie, 7 • Exotic Chicken Curry, 8 • New England Boiled Dinner, 9 • Red Flannel Hash, 10 • Rinktum-Tiddy, 10 • Boston Baked Beans, 11 • Succotash, 12 • Harvard Beets, 13 • North Truro Blueberry Spice Bread, 13 • Boston Brown Bread, 14 • Vermont Soft Gingerbread—1912, 15 • Indian Pudding, 16 • Apple Pandowdy, 17 • Maine "Slump and Grunt," 18 • Connecticut Strawberry/Rhubarb Pie, 19 • Boston Cream Pie, 20 • Snickerdoodles, 22 • Massachusetts Toll House Chocolate Chip Cookies, 23 • All Seasons Easy Cranberry Sauce, 24 • New England Drinks: Tavern Grog, 25; Mulled New England Cider, 25; Cranberry Cape Codder, 25

The Middle Atlantic   27

Mushrooms à la Russe, 29 • Philly Cheese Steak Sandwich, 30 • Senate Bean Soup, 31 • Roasted Long Island Duck, 31 • New York Chicken Divan, 32 • Capitol Chicken Hash, 33 • Greenwich Village Chicken Cacciatore, 34 • Russian Tea Room Shashlik, 35 • Harlem Barbecue Sauce, 37 • Pennsylvania Waffles, 37 • Waldorf Salad, 38 • Diner Greek Salad, 39 • New York Cole Slaw, 39 • Maryann's Jersey Tomato Salad, 40 • Deli Double Chocolate Cheesecake, 41 • New York Cheesecake, 42 • Shoo-Fly Pie, 43 • Teddy Roosevelt's Christmas Sand Tarts, 44 • Ann's Apple Cake, 45 • Halloween Pumpkin Cupcakes, 46 • Mid-Atlantic Drinks: Philadelphia Winter Punch, 48; New Jersey Egg Nog, 49; The Manhattan, 49

The South   51

Shrimp Remoulade, 54 • Virginia Peanut Soup, 54 • Thomas Jefferson Deviled Crab, 55 • Shrimp Jambalaya, 56 • Myrtle Grove Plantation Gumbo, 57 • Southern Fried Chicken with Cream Gravy, 59 Brunswick Stew, 60 • Pulled Pork Sandwiches, 61 • Hoppin' John, 62 Red Beans and Rice, 63 • Fourth of July Macaroni and Cheese, 64 Baked Virginia Cheese Grits, 65 • Skillet Cornbread, 65 • Kentucky Scramble, 66 • Eggs Sardou, 67 • Pelican Club Mashed Sweet Potatoes, 68 • Delta Queen Bread Pudding, 69 • Brennan's Bananas Foster, 70 • Key Lime Pie, 71 • Savannah Pumpkin Pecan Pie, 72 Ambrosia, 74 • Cooling Southern Drinks: Mint Julep, 75; Sazerac, 75; Ramos Gin Fizz, 76; Cajun Coffee, 76; Southern Summer Lemonade, 77

The Heartland   79

Thanksgiving Roast Turkey with Mushroom Sage Dressing, 80 Cathy's Mom's Great Pork and Sauerkraut, 82 • Milwaukee Beer Beef Party Stew, 82 • Granny's Ham and Potato Gratin for a Crowd, 83 Swiss Steak, 85 • Swedish Meatballs, 86 • Delilah's Utah Casserole, 87 • German Apple Pancakes, 88 • Minnesota Wild Rice with Mushrooms, 89 • Chicago Polish Asparagus, 89 • Golden Glow Salad, 90 • Kansas Potato Salad, 91 • Farm Buttermilk Biscuits, 92 • "The Toasts": Cinnamon, French, and Get-Well Milk, 92 • Indiana Devil's Food Coffee Cake, 94 • Illinois Lincoln Thanksgiving Pumpkin Pie, 95 Wichita Peanut Butter and Jelly Cookies, 96 • All-American Brownies, 97 • Heartland Drinks: Bourbon Highball, 98; Bourbon Press, 99; Whiskey Sour, 99; Tom Collins, 99; Gin Rickey, 99

The Northwest and Alaska   101

Anchorage Broiled Halibut with Olive-Cheese Topping, 103 • Alaska State Fair Barbecued Spareribs, 104 • Steaks with Oregon Blue Cheese Topping, 105 • The All-American Hamburger, 106 • Alaskan Sourdough Starter, 107 • Sourdough Blueberry Pancakes, 108 • Seattle Art Museum's Salade Niçoise Northwest, 109 • Baked Alaska, 111 Washington Apple Pie, 113 • Coffee Cinnamon Chocolate Chip Bars, 114 • Rogue Valley Poached Pears, 115 • Northwestern Drinks: Seattle Hot Cocoa, 116; Oregon Celebration Raspberry Punch, 116; Bloody Mary, 117; Kenai Campfire Coffee, 117

The Southwest   119

Georgia O'Keeffe Watercress Soup, 121 • Santa Fe Gazpacho, 121
Tortilla Soup, 122 • New Mexico Albondigas Soup, 123 • Party
Posole, 124 • Taos Enchiladas, 125 • San Antonio River Walk
Enchiladas, 126 • Texas Chili, 128 • Texas Chicken-fried Steak, 129
Santa Fe Jalapeño Cheese Muffins, 130 • Rio Hondo Autumn Pear
Salad, 131 • Texas Ranch-style Dressing, 132 • San Antonio Pecan
Pie, 133 • Canyon Road Spicy Crunch Cookies, 133 • Favorite Drinks
for Hot Summers and Cold Winters: Margaritas, 134; White Sangria,
135; Texas Iced Tea, 135

The West   137

Celery Victor, 139 • San Pedro Marinated Vegetables, 140 • Las Vegas
Shrimp Cocktail, 141 • Sonoma Spinach-filled Hard-boiled Eggs, 142
Yellow Squash Soup with M.F.K. Fisher, 142 • Fisherman's Wharf
Cioppino, 144 • Idaho Rainbow Trout, 145 • Zesty Catalina Swordfish,
146 • Rancho Days Fiesta Enchiladas, 147 • Luisa Tetrazzini's
Chicken and Pasta Casserole, 148 • Les Guthrie's Mother's Meat Loaf,
149 • Los Angeles Tamale Pie, 151 • America's Favorite: Hot Dogs,
152 • Chinese Eggs Foo Yung, 154 • Everyday Lunch Tuna
Sandwiches, 155 • California Mission Days Green Chile Rice, 155
San Francisco Stir-fried Asparagus, 156 • Idaho Perfect Baked Potatoes
and Variations, 157 • Cafe Hash Browns, 158 • Cobb Salad from Los
Angeles, 159 • Hollywood Bowl Pasta Salad, 160 • D.D.'s Ceres
Carrot-Raisin Salad, 161 • Snake Basin Idaho Applesauce, 162
California Lemon Snow Bars, 162 • Golden Gate Rum Pie, 164
Drugstore Banana Split, 164 • Classic Western Drinks: California-style
Martini, 166; Irish Coffee, 166; Orange Brunch Sangria, 167

Hawaii   169

Island Rumaki, 171 • Portuguese Bean Soup, 171 • Maui Onion Soup,
172 • Baked Opakapaka in Orange Citrus Sauce, 173 • Hawaiian
Pineapple-Beef Skewers, 174 • Island-style Steak Teriyaki, 174
Polynesian-flavored Brisket, 175 • Diamond Head Sunset Papaya Salad,
176 • Hanalei Bay Chicken Salad, 177 • Pineapple Cornbread Muffins,
177 • Paradise Banana Bread, 178 • Pineapple Upside-down Cake, 179
Waikiki Coconut Cream Pie, 180 • Cool Island Drinks: Mike's Mai Tai,
181; Piña Colada, 182; Waikiki Frozen Pineapple Daiquiri, 182;
Honolulu Sunset Cooler Punch, 182

Index, 183

ACKNOWLEDGMENTS

For a mother, Mary Macy Staats, who gave me free reign of the kitchen and a father, Irving Anderson Eckhoff, who cared about my spelling and adored my cooking. Gratitude to my Grandpa Henry Taylor Staats who lovingly read me *The National Geographic* when I was only three—and sowed forever the seeds of my passion for travel. For "Nana," Lilla Wilkinson, who shared her Southern life and cooking secrets. Thanks to a loyal sister, Barbara Ellen Hall, who shares our happy childhood memories of love and food.

Foremost, grateful thanks to my computer mentor and master proofreader, Steve Hoffmann, for generous time and sage advice. To dear friends who assisted with recipes: Joan and Hal Clark, Les and Maryann Guthrie, Ann and Ed Kitt, Kriss Erickson, Cathy Zadel, and Peggy Perry. To my writer friend Hillary Hauser for literary advice. To Julia Child for peppy inspiration. Special thanks to the late M.F.K. Fisher for friendship and discerning advice with my writing endeavors.

For helping with recipe tasting, my children's spouses, Dana, Susanne, and Sepp, along with our grandchildren, Gordon, Evelyn, Zachary, and Alex. Thanks to my editor Toni King for caring editing. Lastly, love and appreciation to the late Timothy Purpus for lively encouragement in my teaching and writing.

FOREWORD

The United States has to be one of the best places in the world to live if you love food. Due to the diversity of ethnic groups that make up this beautiful country, almost everything you could possibly imagine is at your fingertips. With the convenience of telephone, facsimile, and computer ordering, literally nothing is unattainable.

Remember Mom and your favorite aunt in the kitchen cooking that delicious meatloaf for all the family to sit down to after a long day of softball in the yard? The smell of an apple pie cooling in the window, tempting you to the point of putting your finger in it without leaving a trace so Mom would not know? These are the foods that people seem to be coming back to.

While all of us did not grow up in the Midwest, we all have our own "homestyle" foods. I grew up in New York, under foot of my wonderful Italian grandmother. I remember her kitchen as the focal point of my existence. The smell of fresh tomatoes and herbs simmering on the stove, and Grandma rolling out the dough for the fresh pasta we would all enjoy, are some of my fondest memories. Just down the street, my friends were sitting down at their table for some knockwurst and sauerkraut. Next door, the Cohen family was sitting down at their table for beef brisket and kasha. We all have our own food memories that stir those special thoughts in the back of our minds.

In my teens, I moved to Los Angeles—the City of Angels or the city of "anything goes." The memories of my grandmother's kitchen never left my mind, and I found myself working in a restaurant. It was not enough to be out front with the diners; I had to jump into the trenches and get right into the process of preparing food. It is because of my love of food and my crazy imagination that I started combining different ethnic tastes and foods to come up with some exciting new dishes.

To get new ideas and find new inspiration, you must venture out and travel around the country. This cookbook has done just that, so you need not leave the comforts of your own home. It amazes me how very different the regions and states can be in regard to their styles of food.

I was the chef at a restaurant in the small beach community of Hermosa Beach, California, where I had the extreme privilege of meeting Betty Evans. This nice, friendly lady could be seen in the dining room at least once a week. We started a conversation one day, and to my surprise, I found out that she was a chef and the food editor of the local paper. On many occasions she would stop in the kitchen with special herbs or vegetables from her garden, to share a recipe, or just to see what was cooking. Our love of food and the enjoyment we share in preparing it for our friends and customers has built a long-term relationship. I have enjoyed reading all her cookbooks and feel honored that she has included me in this, her newest project.

This joyous celebration of the best of American cooking should inspire us all to jump into the kitchen and whip up some time-honored meals. When was the last time you made a Boston Cream Pie or Chicken Divan? Have you ever tried a Southern favorite like Shrimp Jambalaya, or ventured to the Southwest for Taos Enchiladas? Betty brings all of this to you in a user-friendly format. Thank you, Betty, from a great fan.

Robert Bell
Chef and co-owner: Chez Melange,
Depot, Descanso, Fino, Misto,
Pier Avenue Bakery, and Chez

PREFACE

O Beautiful for spacious skies,
For amber waves of grain,
For purple mountain majesties
Above the fruited plain!

America! America!
God shed His grace on thee
And crowned thy good with brotherhood
From sea to shining sea!

During the time I was writing this cookbook, my granddaughter Evelyn graduated from the fifth grade. As part of the ceremony, a youthful school band played this nostalgic American song. The audience, young and old, sang enthusiastically, and the simple words and melodic beauty filled me with patriotic sentiment. I reflected on the many alluring American sites I had visited, and the delicious foods I had tasted, while collecting recipes for this book.

It is satisfying to discover that American cooking is very much alive, in spite of diets, restaurant franchises, health worries, and hurried schedules. Men and women are having fun taking cooking classes, watching televised food programs, and searching for culinary information on the Internet. There is a renewed interest in seeking out old family recipes. The focus on American cooking is evident in every city. Restaurants offer dishes unique to our nation, and to their own regions, on their menus. Across America, "farmers' markets" are appearing and growing for customers who desire just-picked vegetables and fruits. Americans are rediscovering the joy of homestyle cooking.

I am confident that these recipes will not be intimidating for any cook. It is my hope that this book will encourage you to invite friends, new and old, to share a lunch or dinner with you. There is an intense, captivating warmth in cooking and dining friendships.

NEW ENGLAND

New England is one of the most picturesque regions of the country, with pristine white-spired churches set in the middle of charming villages. Rock walls curl about tall, leafy trees that in autumn burst into blazing colors. The Eastern coast is craggy and rugged, with a tradition of brave, strong fishermen who not only fish the bountiful Georges Bank but sail far away to distant seas. Winters are harsh and provide the inspiration for hearty chowders, warming one-pot dinners, and the renowned baked beans (religious rules forbidding work on the Sabbath created the need for New England baked beans to be baked on Saturday and kept warm in brick ovens for Sunday dinner). Abundant seafood provides flavorful ingredients for beach clambakes. Plentiful berries of various kinds make berry-picking parties a local recreation.

My first interest in New England was kindled by my grandmother's sister Violet who resided in Vermont. At Christmas, she would mail us a can of real maple syrup. The label had a drawing of a man tapping the trees for syrup. My mother would make waffles from scratch in her sturdy black waffle iron. I would put on a pat of butter and then generously dribble on this thick, fragrant syrup. It was very pleasurable.

My most personal encounter with New England was in my early married years. We spent a summer on Cape Cod as Gordon attended the Jerry Farnsworth School of Art in North Truro. Reasonable summer rentals were hard to find. Through the school, we found a kind of maid's two-story small carriage house behind a (we were told very legendary) sea captain's house. I could walk to the nearby scallop processing factory where it was possible to buy "second" scallops for minimal cost. These scallops were slightly misshapen but retained perfect flavor. I quickly learned to use them in many ways. Some afternoons after school, we fished for striped bass. Gordon painted old weathered boats and forsaken empty houses on sand dunes. I made all kinds of blueberry creations with our "free" hand-picked berries. Too soon, the Cape Cod summer ended.

The beauty of New England cooking is in its honest simplicity, laced with a little frugality and the heritage of our nation's modest beginnings.

Paula's Mystic Hot Crab Dip

Mystic, a historic seaport in Connecticut, was a nineteenth-century shipbuilding and whaling town. Seamen left from here on very lengthy voyages to gather whale oil from every sea. Today, Mystic is filled with tourists who can board the celebrated old sailing ships, have a fresh seafood meal, and shop for souvenirs and antiques. My friend Joan's daughter, Paula, married a man from Mystic, and now she and her family live in this fascinating town. Paula sent me this delicious recipe for the local hot crab dip. Many New England inns and taverns offer this sort of thing as an appetizer to guests awaiting dinner.

- 1 8-ounce package cream cheese, at room temperature
- 1 6-ounce can good-quality crab meat, drained (or 1 cup fresh or imitation crab meat)
- 1 tablespoon horseradish
- 2 tablespoons milk
- 2 tablespoons finely chopped white onion or 2 minced green onions
-    freshly ground black pepper to taste
- 2 tablespoons bread crumbs
-    paprika for garnish

Combine all ingredients except bread crumbs and paprika. Blend well and place in a small ovenproof dish. Sprinkle with bread crumbs and paprika. Bake at 350° for 20 minutes. This makes about 2 cups. Serve with crackers. I had some of this dip left over and used it as a stuffing for chiles rellenos. It is a most tasty combination.

Corn Chowder

The name "chowder" originates from the French word *chaudiere,* which translates as "iron pot." For the first colonists, this was the essential pot for cooking. On those cold, blustery New England evenings, corn chowder made a most satisfying dinner.

- ½ cup salt pork, cut into ¼-inch dice
- ½ cup diced onion (one small onion)
- 3 cups peeled, diced potatoes
- 1 cup diced celery
- 1 cup water
- salt and pepper to taste
- 2 cups milk or half-and-half
- 2 cups fresh, frozen, or canned corn kernels
- minced parsley for garnish

In a soup pot, fry the salt pork over a medium flame until lightly browned and the fat begins to fry out. Add the onion and fry with the salt pork until onion is limp. Add the potatoes, celery, water, salt, and pepper. Cover and cook until potatoes are tender, about 35 minutes. Add the milk and corn and heat together over a low flame until the corn is tender, about 10 minutes.

Garnish with parsley. Serves 6.

Boston Clam Chowder

Boston clam chowder is made with a milk/cream base, and Manhattan clam chowder has a tomato base. Naturally, there are debates over which is better. Take your choice; both are delicious! However, if you should ever find yourself enjoying a steaming bowl of Boston chowder in a weather-fortified New England house, with a warming fireplace and a northeaster blowing outside, it will instantly become your favorite.

- 2 tablespoons butter
- 2 slices bacon or salt pork, diced
- 1 medium chopped onion
- 3 cups peeled, diced potatoes
- 1 cup dry white wine
- 1 cup cream or half-and-half
- 1 cup milk
- 1 7-ounce can chopped clams (or 1 cup fresh diced clams or fish)
- salt and pepper to taste

Melt the butter in a 2-quart soup pot. Add the bacon and onion, and cook just until very lightly browned. Add the juice from the can of clams (if used), the wine, and the potatoes. If you are using fresh clams or fish, add an extra cup of liquid (water, wine, or milk). Add salt and pepper to taste. Cover and cook until potatoes are tender, about 20 minutes. Remove cover and add clams or fish with the milk and cream. Heat thoroughly, but do not boil. Serve to 4, garnished with a little minced parsley and chowder crackers.

East Coast Steamed Lobster

It certainly does seem like a fantasy to hear that when the colonists first settled in coastal New England, lobsters were so plentiful that farmers would plow them into their fields for fertilizer. Today they are a luxury to be served at the most special dinners. *Homarus americanus* is a uniquely succulent lobster found only along America's east coast. In our local California supermarkets, these Eastern lobsters are often flown in for special promotions. They are alive and wiggling. I could not resist them for a New Year's Eve celebration. With a glass of bubbly champagne, there certainly can be no better way to begin the new year.

Our long-time New York friends Ann and Ed are lobster experts. We have shared many lobster dinners with them in rustic Long Island seafood restaurants. When the waiters ask how we want them prepared, Ed always says "steamed!" He explains that this is the only way to prepare a local lobster, as this method preserves all the delectable flavor and texture. Often, he will ask to see the lobsters before they are cooked—a sight which can surely stir up one's appetite. Ed prefers lobsters weighing just under 3 pounds. Heeding our friend's advice, I prepared our New Year's feast just as he recommended.

2 live Maine lobsters (2–3 pounds each)
  large pot (6–8-quart)
  salted water, or seawater if available
  melted butter for dipping
  lemon wedges

Rinse lobsters quickly under cool running water. Carefully remove rubber bands from their claws. Heat 2 inches of water in the pot. When it is boiling rapidly, lay the lobsters in the water on their backs. Cook, covered, over medium-high flame for 20 minutes from the time the water returns to a boil. Remove from pot with tongs and serve immediately on warmed plates with melted butter and lemon wedges. This will serve 2. Don't forget the bibs and champagne!

Don's Oyster Stew

"Come over for some oyster stew and champagne!" This was a favorite impromptu form of entertainment by our neighbor Don. This classic East Coast dish, perfect for chilly evenings around a fire, is pure and simple, without any frills, and can be made easily and quickly.

Do not be afraid of oysters. These beautiful, glistening, slippery mollusks baffle some people who have not had much experience with these flavorful creatures. Oysters have been a cherished food for as long as there have been people on the planet to enjoy them. Casanova ate fifty a day as "a spur to the spirit and to love." Diamond Jim Brady liked to devour at least five dozen before ordering dinner. Oysters contain many vitamins and minerals, and the Oyster Institute of America's slogan is "Eat oysters—love longer!"

- 8 ounces shelled fresh Eastern oysters, or Western, or canned
- 3 tablespoons butter
- 1 cup milk
- 1 cup half-and-half or cream
- 1 tablespoon white wine
-   salt and pepper to taste
-   paprika for garnish
-   oyster crackers

Melt butter in a heavy soup pot or saucepan. Drain the oysters, saving the liquid. Drop the oysters in the butter and stir around for a minute. Add milk, half-and-half, wine, salt, pepper, and oyster liquid. Heat slowly, but do not boil (you only want the stew to be hot). Ladle into two soup bowls and garnish with a dash of paprika. Serve with oyster crackers. This stew is thin, and that is why you add the crackers. This will serve 2 for a cozy evening meal.

Cape Cod Clam Pie

"Clam pies for sale" is a familiar sign along winding Cape Cod roads where housewives and local grocery stores are in the pie business. The pies are available in several sizes. The small ones are perfect for a mid-morning pick-up or a light lunch. The larger ones can be used for a beach picnic or casual dinner. The recipe may seem a little "plain," but remember, New Englanders like simple, honest food. They have lived well for many years on potatoes and seafood.

- 2 6-ounce cans minced clams (or 2 cups fresh chopped clams)
- 4 slices bacon or salt pork, diced
- 1 medium onion or 4 green onions, minced
- 3–4 peeled, diced raw potatoes
- salt and pepper to taste
- 1 teaspoon paprika
- 2 tablespoons white wine (optional)
- ½ cup half-and-half
- dab of butter for pan

In a frying pan, fry the bacon or salt pork until light brown. Add onions, potatoes, salt, pepper, and paprika, and stir-fry for 10 minutes. Add wine, half-and-half, and drained clams. Place in a lightly buttered 10-inch pie pan (or something similar). Cover with top crust and bake at 400° for 30 minutes. This will serve 4.

Basic Top Piecrust

- 1 cup flour
- ⅓ cup shortening
- 1 teaspoon salt
- cold milk

Sift flour and salt together; add shortening and blend with pastry cutter or fork until the mixture resembles coarse meal. Add milk until dough sticks together. Form into a ball and roll out on a floured surface. Place over the clam mixture. Prick the top with a fork in a few places.

Exotic Chicken Curry

While New England cooking is basically simple, using local ingredients, here as everywhere there exists a desire for exotic flavors. Often, the men were away for years on sailing voyages. When they returned to their New England home ports, they would bring curry powder from faraway tropical lands. The New England ladies would go all out and prepare a curry party.

- 2 tablespoons olive oil or butter
- 2 cooking apples, peeled and cored
- 1 green pepper, seeded
- 2 onions
- 1 tablespoon curry powder
- 2 tablespoons flour
- salt and pepper to taste
- 1½ cups chicken stock
- ½ cup white wine
- 1 lemon (juice and grated rind)
- 2 cups cooked, cubed chicken (can be mixture of thighs and breasts)
- steamed rice

Condiments

- chopped peanuts
- minced green onions
- crumbled cooked bacon
- chopped hard-boiled egg
- chutney
- grated coconut

Heat oil or butter in a large pot. Coarsely chop the apples, pepper, and onions together. Add to pot and stir just until limp. Blend in the curry powder. Add stock, wine, and lemon. Simmer uncovered for 15 minutes over a low flame. Add chicken and cook an additional 15 minutes.

Serve with hot steamed rice. Place the condiments in individual small pretty bowls so guests can help themselves. Fresh sliced or cubed tropical fruits such as pineapple, papaya, mango, or melon may also be served. This will serve 4 and can be easily doubled or tripled for a large curry party.

New England Boiled Dinner

This is a most hearty and satisfying dinner. For those early New England women, this was a dinner of expediency. The cooking was accomplished in a large iron pot (most likely the only pot in the household), in the fireplace. The housewife just added ingredients as desired.

- 3–4 pounds corned beef, brisket cut
- salt and pepper to taste
- 4 medium onions, peeled
- 4 medium carrots, cut in thirds
- 2 turnips, peeled and cubed
- 4 medium potatoes, peeled, or 8 small new or red potatoes
- 1 medium cabbage, quartered
- 4 medium beets (optional)

Place the brisket in a large pot. Cover with cold water; add salt and pepper. Cover and simmer over a low flame until tender. (This can also be cooked in the oven at 350°.) The brisket will take 2 to 2½ hours to become tender. In the last hour, add the onions, carrots, turnips, and potatoes. If any of the vegetables are tender before the hour is up, remove and keep warm; you do not want squishy overcooked vegetables. In the last thirty minutes, mound the cabbage on top of the brisket. The beets should be cooked separately, covered with salted water in a covered saucepan, until tender—about 25 minutes. Peel the beets when done and arrange on a platter with the meat, surrounded by the vegetables. This will serve 4. Any leftovers can be made into "Red Flannel Hash."

Red Flannel Hash

New England ladies had to be practical and thrifty with their cooking time. "New England boiled dinner" leftovers could easily be turned into the next day's "red flannel hash," so called because the beets give a fresh reddish glow to the hash. In the mountains of Vermont, this was a popular dish with Ethan Allen and his Green Mountain Boys. This modern version is easy and most satisfying.

4	medium potatoes, cooked, peeled, and chopped (about 3 cups)
6	medium beets, cooked, peeled, and chopped (about 1½ cups)
1½	cups cooked corned beef brisket, cut in small pieces
3	green onions, minced
	salt and pepper to taste
¼	cup liquid: red wine, stock, or milk
¼	cup bacon drippings, butter, oil, or a combination of these
	eggs, 1 or 2 per person (optional)
	parsley for garnish
	red pepper sauce (optional)

Combine all ingredients except the last four in a bowl and mix thoroughly. Heat the drippings in a frying pan until hot. Place the hash in the pan and pat down with a spatula. Cook for 15 minutes and turn over, moving so that the crispy parts mingle with the hash, then cook for another 15 minutes. Serve to 3 on warmed plates. If desired, eggs may be broken (like fried eggs) over the hash; cover and cook until the eggs are firm. Garnish with parsley and dapple a few drops of hot sauce on top if you want.

Rinktum-Tiddy

Rinktum-Tiddy is a cozy, comfortable New England creation. It is a perfect aid for recovery from a cold or hangover, and children who do not enjoy complicated adult food adore it. In Vermont, it is a favorite warm supper dish for chilly evenings.

2	tablespoons butter
2	green onions, finely minced
1	tablespoon flour
1	16-ounce can whole peeled tomatoes
1½	cups grated cheddar cheese
1	egg, beaten
	salt and pepper to taste
	pinch of cayenne pepper (optional)
6	slices buttered toast of your choice

Melt the butter. Add the onions and lightly fry just until limp. Add the flour and blend. Place the tomatoes in a bowl and break them up into small pieces with a fork or scissors. Slowly add the tomatoes to the pan and mix with the sautéed onions. Next add the cheese, stirring over a low flame. Blend in the egg, salt, and pepper, stirring until mixture is smooth. Pour over hot buttered toast. Serve at once to 2 or 3.

Boston Baked Beans

The Pilgrims baked their beans on Saturday because of the religious mandate that dictated Sunday as a day of rest. They baked them overnight in brick ovens, but with today's modern stoves, baked beans can easily be prepared in 4 hours. Baking beans is a wonderful kitchen experience, as appetizing scents fill the house. You can bake brown bread at the same time, just as the efficient New England ladies did.

2	cups (1 pound) small white beans
½	pound salt pork
1	teaspoon dry mustard or 2 teaspoons Dijon-style mustard
⅓	cup dark brown sugar
¼	cup molasses
1	onion, diced
	salt and pepper to taste

New research indicates that soaking beans is not necessary. The cooking time may be a little longer as a consequence, but the flavor will be more intense.

Place the beans in a large pot. Cover with 4 quarts water and 1 teaspoon salt. Cover and simmer until just barely tender, about 1 hour. (Old purists say "until you can blow away the skins," which the eminent cookbook writer Fanny Farmer explains thusly: "Taking a few beans on the tip of a spoon, blow on them; the skins will burst if sufficiently cooked. Beans thus tested must of course be thrown away." Other Boston writers simply say to cook until the bean skins wrinkle and crack.)

Drain the beans, reserving the liquid. Cut slits in the pork rind to prevent it from curling. Place the pork in a bean pot and cover with 3 quarts of the reserved liquid; stir in mustard, salt, pepper, onion, molasses, and brown sugar. Add beans, placing the salt pork deep in the center. Bake at 300°, covered, for 3 hours, stirring now and then and adding additional reserved bean liquid as necessary.

Remove cover and bring salt pork to the top to brown. Cook an additional hour. This will serve 8.

Succotash

Succotash is a most attractive dish, delicious and full of exciting textures and flavors. Corn was the colonists' first vegetable. Native Americans taught them how to plant and harvest the corn, which surely made it possible for them to survive their first years in the new world. The Indian word for boiled corn was *m'sickquatash*. The settlers added beans and called the mixture "succotash." The best is made with tiny fresh lima beans and fresh corn scraped from the cob. In the winter, a quite acceptable version can be made with frozen beans and corn. Some cooks use string beans instead of limas.

- 2 cups fresh shelled lima beans (or 1 10-ounce package frozen)
- 2 cups fresh corn kernels (4–5 ears cut from the cob, or 1 10-ounce package frozen)
- 2 tablespoons butter
- salt and pepper to taste
- ¼ cup cream
- 2 tablespoons white wine (optional)

Cook fresh beans in salted water to cover until tender, about 12 minutes. Cook fresh corn separately in the same way, about 5 minutes. (If using frozen vegetables, cook according to package directions.) Drain both vegetables and return together to a saucepan. Add salt, pepper, butter, cream, and wine. Heat just until hot. Do not boil. This will serve 4–5.

Harvard Beets

Beets prepared with this tangy sauce are called "Harvard beets," because red is that school's color (a similar recipe for "Yale beets" substitutes orange juice for the vinegar). Beets are healthy, delicious, and always plentiful.

    3   cups beets, cooked, peeled, and sliced
    ½   cup sugar
    1½   teaspoons cornstarch
    ¼   cup water
    ¼   cup white cider vinegar
    2   tablespoons butter

You will need 4 medium-sized beets for this recipe. To cook them, remove all but two inches of the stems, rinse off any dirt, and place the beets in a pot large enough not to crowd them. Cover with salted water and cook gently until tender, about 45 minutes. Cool and slip off the skins before slicing.

Combine sugar, cornstarch, water, and vinegar in a saucepan. Cook over a low flame, stirring, until slightly thick. Add butter and blend. Add beets and heat to serving temperature. This serves 4–5.

North Truro Blueberry Spice Bread

Picking blueberries on a sultry summer day, with assorted insects flitting around you, is an absorbing experience. We used to pick blueberries in North Truro while Gordon was attending a Cape Cod art school. Fresh from California, we soon saw that the locals knew all the places where the picking was easy and bountiful. One afternoon as we were visiting the town graveyard to read the old epitaphs, I noticed that there were plump unpicked blueberries along the fence. This spot became our private preserve, where we gathered many, many berries. In my tiny kitchen (a former maid's quarters) I made pies and muffins and this easy bread. Any kind of blueberries can be used, but if you are in New England and can find a spot to pick your own berries, they will certainly be the very best.

- 1½ cups fresh or frozen blueberries
- ½ cup oil (canola or vegetable)
- 1 cup sugar, white or brown
- ¼ cup molasses
- 1 egg
- 2 cups flour
- ½ teaspoon salt
- 1 teaspoon ginger
- 1 teaspoon cinnamon
- ½ teaspoon nutmeg
- 1 teaspoon baking soda
- 1 cup buttermilk
- 1 tablespoon grated orange or lemon rind

Mix together the oil, sugar, and molasses by hand or with an electric beater until smooth. Beat in egg. Sift dry ingredients together. Remove 2 tablespoons of this mixture and blend with the blueberries—this helps to evenly distribute them within the bread. Add dry ingredients, alternately with buttermilk, to the oil/egg mixture, beating after each addition. Gently stir in the blueberries and rind. Pour into a greased 12″ x 7½″ x 2″ baking dish and bake at 350° for 40 minutes. Cool on a rack for 5 minutes and cut into slices or squares of desired size.

Boston Brown Bread

Hot, fragrant brown bread is the traditional, and best, accompaniment for Boston baked beans. My mother often prepared this typically American supper in our Los Angeles home, even though she had never been to Boston. She simply used canned bread and canned Boston baked beans.

It was always satisfying, but baking this bread in coffee cans is a fun adventure and the bread is splendid.

Molasses was the "sugar" of the colonists and helped fortify them against the cold, dour, endless winters. Preheated brick ovens were used for the settlers' baking. These efficient old ovens may be seen today in historic New England houses.

- 1 cup rye flour
- 1 cup white flour
- 1 cup wheat flour
- 2 teaspoons baking soda
- 1 teaspoon salt
- 1 cup white or yellow cornmeal
- 2 cups buttermilk
- 2 tablespoons melted butter plus 2 additional tablespoons for greasing mold
- ¾ cup molasses
- 1 cup raisins

Sift dry ingredients (except cornmeal) together, then blend in cornmeal. Combine milk, melted butter, and molasses, then blend with the dry ingredients and mix in the raisins. Lightly rub two 1-quart coffee cans (or similar containers) with butter. Fill cans with batter up to two-thirds full. (You can also use an 8-cup pudding mold.) Place cans on a metal rack or trivet in a large kettle. Fill the kettle with enough water to reach about 3 inches up the sides of the cans, and cover. Steam for 2½ to 3 hours, adding additional water to keep it at about the same level. Remove and let stand 10 minutes in the cans before unmolding. This will make two loaves or one large molded bread.

Vermont Soft Gingerbread–1912

Ginger is used in many ways in New England, and gingerbread is one of the favorites. In some New England states, there used to be a sort of holiday known as "Muster Day" when the local men would come to town for militia training. Fortunately, not much time was spent on this drudgery. The highlight of the event was eating gingerbread, sold by vendors and accompanied by rum. This recipe was a favorite of a Vermont grand-aunt.

- 2 cups flour
- 2 teaspoons baking powder
- ½ teaspoon baking soda
- ¼ cup sugar
- ½ teaspoon salt
- 2 teaspoons ginger
- 1 teaspoon cinnamon
- 1 egg
- ½ cup milk
- ½ cup molasses
- ¼ cup melted butter

Sift the dry ingredients together. Beat the egg in a bowl; add milk and molasses. Stir into the flour mixture. Add melted butter and combine well. Pour into a well-greased loaf pan and bake at 350° for 30 minutes. The batter may also be poured into cupcake or muffin tins, where the baking will take 20–25 minutes.

Indian Pudding

This simple, flavorful pudding was certainly one of the first desserts of the colonists. The origin of the name is that cornmeal came from "Indian corn" as distinguished from wheat (the British called wheat "corn"). Because wheat flour was scarce, the New Englanders learned to use this "Indian meal." The earliest recipe for this dessert was from our first cookbook lady, Amelia Simmons, in 1796. She called it "a nice Indian pudding." At Boston's Durgin Park restaurant, this pudding is available every day.

4	cups milk (reserve one cup for topping)
2	tablespoons butter
⅓	cup cornmeal, yellow or white
½	cup molasses
1	egg, beaten
¼	cup sugar
½	teaspoon salt
½	teaspoon ginger
½	teaspoon cinnamon
¼	teaspoon nutmeg

In a heavy saucepan, heat 3 cups of the milk with the butter until bubbles appear around the edge of the pan. Slowly stir in the cornmeal and molasses. Cook over a low flame, stirring constantly until thickened—about 10 minutes. Remove from heat and blend in the beaten egg. Stir in remaining ingredients and mix together.

Place in a buttered 1-quart baking dish. Float the remaining 1 cup of milk over the top, but do not stir. Bake at 300° for 2 to 2½ hours. The pudding will firm as it cools. Serve slightly warm with ice cream or whipped cream topping if desired; it may also be served cold. This will serve 6.

Sometimes, in modern versions of this classic dessert, ½ cup raisins or about 1 tablespoon grated rind of orange is added.

Note: The colonists cooked Indian pudding in their brick ovens along with brown bread and baked beans.

Apple Pandowdy

Apple pandowdy starts out as an apple pie with only a top crust. After the pie is baked, the crust is broken up ("dowdy" is an old word meaning "untidy"!) into the apple filling. It is a homey, happy, easy dessert and always pleasing. A Maine legend has it that Eve made the first apple pandowdy and Adam fell for it.

Pie Filling

    4   apples, preferably tart ones
    ½   cup sugar
    ½   teaspoon cinnamon
    2   tablespoons butter

Peel, core, and thinly slice the apples. Place in a shallow baking dish, sprinkle with sugar and cinnamon, and dot with butter.

Crust

    2   cups flour
    3   tablespoons baking powder
    ½   teaspoon salt
    4   tablespoons butter or shortening
    ¾   cup milk
         whipping cream for topping

Sift the dry ingredients together. Add butter (or shortening) and mix in with a fork. Add milk to form a soft dough. Place on a floured board and roll out ½ inch thick to fit the baking pan.

Lay the crust over the top of the filling, cutting several gashes to let steam escape. Bake 30 minutes at 350°.

To serve, "dowdy" the crust by breaking it with a sharp knife while warm and mixing it with the apples. Serve warm with thick unbeaten cream. This will serve 4. The cream for topping may also be sweetened with maple syrup and dusted with nutmeg.

A "cob pie" is pandowdy sweetened with molasses instead of sugar.

Maine "Slump and Grunt"

This quaint and unique name is derived from the behavior of men in Maine (and perhaps other states) who consume this dish as a finish to lunch or dinner, and then just want to "slump and grunt" and not return to work. In Maine, a rocking chair on the porch is a favorite place for this slumping and grunting. There are several variations of this recipe, and this oven method seems the best.

	butter for pan
12	ounces fresh blueberries (about 1½ cups)
⅔	cup sugar plus 1 tablespoon
¼	teaspoon nutmeg
1	cup flour
2	teaspoons baking powder
¼	teaspoon salt
¼	cup shortening
⅓	cup milk
	whipping cream for topping (optional)

Lightly butter an 8″ x 8″ baking dish. Mix the blueberries with ⅔ cup sugar and nutmeg. Place in the baking dish. In a bowl, mix the flour, baking powder, salt, and 1 tablespoon sugar. Work in the shortening with a pastry blender or fork, then blend in the milk.

Toss on a floured board. Pat together and then roll dough about ¼ inch thick. Cut in circles or any desired shape and place on top of the blueberries. Bake at 400° until top is brown, about 20 minutes. This is best served warm. In Maine, thick cream (may be whipped) is served on top. This will serve 6.

Connecticut Strawberry/Rhubarb Pie

In colonial times, pies were a big part of each New England meal. The colonists' brick ovens were classified by size as a "10-pie oven" or a "20-pie oven." Pies were practical as a handy, easy-to-eat food that could be taken on sailing voyages or into the farm fields. Housewives would bake many pies at once, then freeze them in the snow or store them in cool cellars.

Rhubarb is known in New England as "pieplant" because it is the first plant to come up in the spring. Strawberries soon follow, so it became popular to combine these two ingredients in a pie. The combined flavors are delicious and very refreshing.

	Pie pastry for a 9-inch, two-crust pie*
2	cups washed and hulled strawberries, halved
2	cups rhubarb, washed, cut into 1-inch pieces
4	tablespoons flour
1¼	cups sugar
¼	teaspoon nutmeg
1	teaspoon grated orange rind (optional)
2	tablespoons butter

Combine the strawberries and rhubarb in a bowl. Add flour, sugar, nutmeg, and orange rind (if used) to the bowl and blend together. Place in the piecrust and dot with butter. Carefully put the top crust on and make deep slits in the crust so the steam can escape. Bake at 400° for 35–40 minutes, until the crust is golden brown. Serve lukewarm to 6–8.

Boston Cream Pie

One does not have to be in Boston to enjoy this pie, which is really not a pie at all but a luscious custard-filled cake cut in wedges like a pie. I was once employed in the personnel office of Bullock's department store, in the heart of downtown Los Angeles. The office workers had a favorite sort of lunch-tea room on Olive Street, where one of the dessert specialties was Boston cream pie. I could never resist it. There is something about the creamy filling between the light cakes and the shiny chocolate glaze that I find addictive.

This cake-pie has been on the menu of the Parker House hotel in Boston since 1856. Such famous American writers as Longfellow, Emerson, Hawthorne, and Whittier met in this hotel for literary discussions and Boston cream pie.

An alternate version of this dessert, wherein raspberry jam is generously spread between the cakes instead of the cream filling, is known as "Washington pie."

---

*For basic piecrust recipe, see "Washington Apple Pie" in The Northwest and Alaska section.

Sponge Cake

Any 2-egg cake may be used, but this easy sponge cake is especially good.

- 4 eggs
- 2 cups sugar
- 2 teaspoons vanilla or rum
- 1 cup milk
- 2 tablespoons butter
- 2 cups flour
- ½ teaspoon salt
- 2 teaspoons baking powder

Beat eggs with electric mixer until very light. Blend in sugar and vanilla or rum. Heat milk to boiling point with butter (until butter is melted). Sift the flour, salt, and baking powder together. Pour milk and butter quickly into eggs and blend. Next blend in flour mixture. Pour right away into two greased and floured 9-inch cake pans. Bake at 350° for 30 minutes. The cake should be golden brown and spring back when touched.

Cream Filling

- 3 tablespoons sugar
- 2 teaspoons cornstarch
- ¼ teaspoon salt
- ¾ cup half-and-half or milk
- 3 egg yolks, beaten lightly in a bowl
- 1 teaspoon vanilla

Mix sugar, cornstarch, and salt together in the top of a double boiler over medium heat. Slowly add milk and blend. Stir constantly until mixture thickens, about 1 minute. Remove about ¼ cup and blend into the egg yolks (this step is necessary because if you add the yolks all at once into the hot mixture, they will curdle). Return egg yolk mixture to the double boiler, add vanilla, and blend. Cool slightly and place in refrigerator until cake is to be assembled.

Chocolate Glaze Topping

- ½ cup semisweet chocolate chips
- 1 tablespoon butter
- 2 tablespoons cold coffee

Melt the chocolate and butter over low heat in a double boiler. Add coffee and stir all ingredients well. Cool slightly before frosting the top of the cake.

Snickerdoodles

Snickerdoodles are the consummate after-school snack. I always liked a glass of milk, or even lemonade, with my snickerdoodles. This cookie is a true American classic, and New England seems to be the origin of the recipe. Somehow it fits in perfectly with those prim and tidy kitchens. This is easy enough to be a perfect cookie project for young children.

- 1 cup shortening (can be half butter)
- 1½ cups sugar plus 3 tablespoons for topping
- 2 eggs
- 2¾ cups white flour
- 1 teaspoon baking soda
- ½ teaspoon salt
- 2 teaspoons cream of tartar
- 1 teaspoon grated lemon peel (optional)
- 1 tablespoon cinnamon

In a mixing bowl, cream the shortening, add the sugar, and mix until light and fluffy. Add the eggs and blend together. Sift the flour, baking soda, salt, and cream of tartar together and blend into the mixture, adding lemon peel if used. Chill dough in bowl for one hour. Roll into balls about the size of walnuts. Mix the cinnamon and 3 tablespoons sugar together in a shallow pan. Roll the balls around in this mixture. Place about 2 inches apart on an ungreased cookie sheet and bake at 400° for 10–12 minutes. Remove from sheet and place on a rack to cool. Store in a covered container. This will make about 48 snickerdoodles.

Massachusetts Toll House Chocolate Chip Cookies

Chocolate chip cookies were certainly not part of the Pilgrims' dessert diet. They did not arrive on the American culinary scene until the late 1930s. Ruth Wakefield, the owner of the Whitman, Massachusetts, Toll House Inn (on the road from Boston to New Bedford), added chopped chocolate to her cookie dough while experimenting with an antiquated recipe of Amelia Simmons'. They were such a big hit that eventually a special machine was developed to mold the chocolate into "chips." The name and recipe were sold to the Nestle Chocolate Company, which prints the original recipe on every bag of chocolate chips. This recipe is a popular variation of the original.

¾	cup butter
¾	cup white sugar
¾	cup brown sugar
2	eggs
3	tablespoons milk
1	teaspoon vanilla
2¼	cups flour
1	teaspoon baking soda
¼	teaspoon salt
1	12-ounce package semisweet chocolate chips
1	cup chopped walnuts or pecans

In a mixing bowl, cream together the butter and sugar. Add the eggs, milk, and vanilla. Sift dry ingredients together. Add to the bowl, and blend well. Stir in the chips and nuts. Drop dough by tablespoonfuls on lightly greased baking sheets. Bake at 375° for 10–12 minutes. Edges should be brown. Remove to a cookie rack and cool. Store in airtight containers. These cookies will freeze very well. This recipe makes about 5 dozen cookies.

All Seasons Easy Cranberry Sauce

The tangy flavor of this native American berry deserves use year-round, not just at Thanksgiving. It tastes delicious with not only poultry but also pork and beef. The word cranberry derives from "crane-berry," an early name given because the pale pink blossoms of the berry look like the head of a crane.

Cranberries were used by Native Americans for medicinal purposes (on arrow wounds as an astringent) and as a dye for fabrics as well as food. Cranberries grow best on peat bogs that are covered with sand. Some Cape Cod vines have been producing for over 150 years. Certainly, cranberries have become a colorful part of American cuisine. The country consumes 340 million pounds of cranberries a year.

- 2 cups water (1 cup red wine or orange juice may be substituted for 1 cup of the water for extra flavor)
- 1½ cups sugar
- 4 cups fresh cranberries, washed

Mix water (or substitute) and sugar together in a saucepan. Simmer for 5 minutes. Add cranberries. Cover and cook until skins pop open, about 4 minutes. Stir to blend. Skim off any froth. Place in a bowl, cool, and refrigerate until needed. This will keep for several weeks and makes about 4½ cups.

New England Drinks

Alcoholic drinks were very much part of the colonist's life. A morning draft of beer was common, served at room temperature as in England. Water was often tainted and difficult to obtain in freezing weather, and the cold, harsh climate created a desire for a warming beverage. Hard apple ciders were popular and were most often the beverage drunk with meals. Hot grog was a favorite winter drink in local taverns.

Tavern Grog

1 jigger rum (light or dark)
1 teaspoon sugar
   hot water to fill glass (about 1 cup)
   lemon slice

Pour the rum and sugar into a glass. Add hot water and lemon slice. Stir well and serve at once.

Mulled New England Cider

Because of the many apple orchards in New England, drinks made with apple cider are local favorites. This one may also be served cool with ice cubes in the summer.

1 quart bottled apple cider
½ cup light brown sugar
2 whole cloves
1 cinnamon stick

Mix ingredients together. Simmer for 10 minutes. Strain and serve in mugs. This will serve 4.

Cranberry Cape Codder

Cranberry juice is refreshing and a beautiful color. At the summer homes on Cape Cod, it is often served with vodka for a cooling summer drink.

2 jiggers cranberry juice
1 jigger vodka
   ice cubes
1 cup club soda

For a "short" drink, the vodka and juice are simply poured over ice cubes. For a "tall," follow the same procedure, adding the soda and giving a stir.

The Middle Atlantic

Not too long ago, I visited Ellis Island. Our New York friends wanted to see it after its recent restoration. We looked at all the exhibits and displays, and saw the film about the immigrants' arrival there. Our friends, whose parents had come to America through Ellis Island, were very touched by this emotional photographic document. Ed's grandfather had fled from Russia, a troop of Cossacks chasing him with drawn swords. Ann's Norwegian father and Bohemian mother had met in New York. Although the immigrants who came to Ellis Island had left their homelands behind, they brought to America their music, literature, crafts, arts, and styles of cooking. A food heritage is an important treasure. It was a comfort, in this new country, to prepare dishes that their families had cooked for generations. These diverse ethnic recipes have made American cuisine unparalleled in the world.

Much of our immigration came through Ellis Island and filtered into the Mid-Atlantic states. (Actually, between 1872 and 1954, around 17 million people passed through Ellis Island.) These states are the homes of many of the nation's liveliest and greatest industrial cities. Some immigrants made fortunes which they used to found and finance museums, parks, and libraries—their generous way of returning something to the country that had given them opportunity.

The cooking characteristic of these states is an intriguing mixture, as are the inhabitants. There is the foundation of the first Dutch, German, and English settlers. Pennsylvania Dutch cooking is really Pennsylvania German, as the German word *deutsch* (meaning "German") was somehow translated as "Dutch." This is good sturdy food with beautiful baked selections. Part of the German heritage is the tradition of sweet and sour relishes. In Pittsburgh, Henry Heinz's 57 Varieties Company was founded upon ketchup and pickles. In Maryland, British seafood favorites became seafood cakes and pies. The Dutch in New York cooked hearty soups and baked crispy cookies. As the immigrants kept arriving, more food riches came. The Jewish contributed their celebrated "deli" sustenance. The Italians settled in the cities and named their neighborhoods "Little Italy"; these neighborhoods are still filled with enticing restaurants and grocery stores infused with arresting scents. African-Americans enriched these cities with their barbecue expertise and succulent "soul food." The Chinese opened restaurants and picturesque gift and provision shops in "Chinatowns." There was a never-ending procession of new citizens into these states, as Puerto Ricans, Irish, Koreans, Japanese, Swiss, Greeks, French, Jamaicans, and others created a true "melting pot."

I have spent a night on a ship returning from Europe, waiting for morning clearance to dock in the port of New York. The city skyline looked like a lit-up, vertical Lego toyland. From the deck, I gazed with delight at the proud Statue of Liberty with her torch shining as a welcome to all, and I was glad to be home.

Mushrooms à la Russe (from New York's Russian Tea Room)

This dish is closely associated with Carnegie Hall, as it is a favorite with concert-goers who want something tasty and filling before they dash next door. If Isaac Stern is playing, he may come in early to enjoy it *en famille*. Faith Stewart-Gordon, the generous owner of the Tea Room, has given me permission to use this delicious Russian recipe.

3–4	quarts water
2	tablespoons salt
2	pounds mushrooms
6	tablespoons butter
½	cup minced onion (1 medium onion)
⅓	cup flour
1	cup milk
1	cup sour cream
1	teaspoon salt or to taste
½	teaspoon freshly ground pepper or to taste
¼	teaspoon Worcestershire sauce
¼	teaspoon ground coriander
½	cup grated Parmesan cheese

Combine water and salt in a large kettle and bring to the boiling point. Meanwhile, trim the mushrooms, place in a bowl, and wash quickly but thoroughly under running water, swishing around with your hands. Drain mushrooms and put them into the boiling water. Cook for no more than 2 minutes after the water has resumed boiling, then drain in a colander. Place drained mushrooms stem-side down on a platter lined with three thicknesses of paper towels to drain further. Pat dry with more paper towels; they must be as dry as possible or the dish will be soupy. Cool mushrooms and slice thinly. Reserve.

Heat butter in a large 10- to 12-inch deep frying pan or shallow saucepan. Add onion and cook over medium heat, stirring constantly for 3 to 5 minutes or until soft; do not brown. Add mushrooms. Cook, stirring all the time, for 3 to 4 minutes. Sprinkle with the flour, toss well, and cook for 2 more minutes. Combine milk and sour cream in a small saucepan and heat, stirring; do not boil. Add to the mushrooms and mix thoroughly. Remove from heat and stir in salt, pepper, Worcestershire sauce, and coriander. Turn into 6 individual baking dishes or a single 10- to 12-cup baking dish. Sprinkle with the Parmesan. Cook in a preheated moderate oven (350°) for 20 minutes or until golden brown and bubbly. Serve hot.

Philly Cheese Steak Sandwich

I have eaten Philly cheese steak sandwiches at fairs in the West, and found the dry meats and stale buns not too exciting. This all changed for me when I was at the Pittsburgh airport, changing planes for a flight to Los Angeles. I noticed a line at the Philly cheese steak concession. Suddenly I felt hungry and joined the line. The cook was stirring succulent pieces of very finely shaved roast beef on a hot griddle with onions. He asked if I wanted mayo, lettuce, and tomato. Yes, I wanted it all and also a bottle of the local beer. The sandwich was marvelous. The meat and onions were flavorful, and all the ingredients were layered in perfect proportions on an excellent bun. I relished every bite. The homey warmth of this American classic makes it a perfect candidate for a cool-day lunch or light supper.

For each sandwich you will need:

> one fresh bun of your choice (usually these are long, about 7 inches, although hamburger buns can also be used)
>
> several thin slices of roast beef (can be leftover roast)
>
> ¼ cup sliced onions
>
> cheese slices (Provolone is a good choice)
>
> lettuce
>
> tomato slices
>
> oil for the grill

Slice onions and lightly brown in a greased frying pan. Add sliced meat and stir until hot. Heat bun just until warm but not toasty; layer beef and onions, cheese, lettuce, and sliced tomatoes on bun. Press together lightly and eat at once.

Senate Bean Soup

Senate Bean Soup is one of the culinary pleasures of the Senate Restaurant in Washington D.C. It is possible for anyone to dine in this capitol restaurant, but you do need to let your senator know ahead of time. My California senator, Dianne Feinstein, was able to help me obtain some of the history of this famed American soup. Its origin is popularly attributed to Senator Fred Thomas Dubois of Idaho, who served in the Senate from 1901 to 1907. While he was chairman of the committee that supervised the Senate restaurant, he gaveled through a resolution requiring that bean soup be on the menu every day.

- 2 pounds small Michigan navy beans (or other)
- 4 quarts hot water
- 1½ smoked ham hocks
- 1 onion, chopped
- 2 tablespoons butter
- salt and pepper to taste

Wash the beans and place in pot of hot water. Add ham hocks and boil slowly for approximately 3½ hours, covered. Stir now and then. Take ham hocks from pot and remove meat. Cut in small pieces and return to soup. Braise onion in butter until light brown, then add to soup. Season to taste with salt and pepper. This will make 8 servings. I have found in some versions of this soup that 1 cup of mashed potatoes is stirred in during the last hour of cooking.

Roasted Long Island Duck

Long Island, that impressive long spit of land that stretches out into the Atlantic, is famed for the Long Island ducks that are raised on special farms. In our colonial times, hunting for wild ducks in the Eastern marshes helped feed the hungry colonists. In 1873, an enterprising sea captain hoping to earn some extra cash brought some White Peking ducks (a popular Chinese domestic duck) from Peking, China, to Long Island. They flourished here, and today this area is one of our nation's largest duck-raising centers. Most restaurants prefer this variety because of the excellent flavor.

1	duck (4–5 pounds)
1	onion, peeled and cut in thirds
1	lemon, quartered
	salt and pepper

Remove neck and "insides" (liver, heart, and gizzard) from duck. These may be covered with 4 cups of water, seasoned with salt and pepper, and simmered for an hour to make stock for gravy, if desired. Remove and dice before adding to gravy.

Pat dry the outside and interior of the duck. Place onion and lemon in the inside. Tie the legs together with string and twist wings under the back. Prick duck with a fork to release the fat. Place duck breast-side-up on a rack. Sprinkle with salt and pepper. Roast for 2–3 hours (30–35 minutes per pound) at 350°. Remove fat from bottom of pan as it accumulates, using a baster. When duck is done, remove to a warmed platter.

For gravy, drain fat from pan (except 2 tablespoons), add 2 tablespoons flour, and with a spatula press the flour down in the pan to absorb duck drippings. Add 2–3 cups stock with additional salt and pepper. Simmer until flour is cooked. Mashed potatoes are superb with this duck gravy. One roast duck will only serve 2–3 persons.

New York Chicken Divan

This nostalgic recipe from the 1920s had its origin at the Divan Parisian restaurant in New York, and Chicken Divan immediately became a sensation across the country. It has stood the test of time and still remains a favorite American recipe.

4	medium chicken breasts (cut in half)
1½	pounds fresh broccoli or 2 packages frozen (10 ounces each)

Easy Hollandaise Sauce

3	tablespoons butter plus 3 tablespoons more
3	tablespoons flour
1½	cups milk
2	egg yolks
3	tablespoons fresh lemon juice
½	cup grated Parmesan cheese

Cover the chicken breasts with lightly salted water and simmer covered until tender, about 25 minutes. Cool in the liquid. Remove the skin and bone. Cut the meat in long thin slices and set aside. (This may be prepared ahead of time.) Trim the broccoli so that you have nice little bite-sized pieces. Steam or simmer in salted water just until tender. Drain and place in a lightly buttered ovenproof baking dish. Carefully lay the chicken slices on top.

To make the sauce, melt 3 tablespoons butter in a heavy saucepan. Add the flour and blend with 3 tablespoons butter. Gradually add milk, stirring to avoid lumps. Cut the remaining 3 tablespoons of butter in tiny pieces and add with the egg yolks. Continue stirring, blending in lemon juice. The sauce should be slightly thick. Pour over chicken. Sprinkle the Parmesan cheese on top. Place about 5 inches under a broiler and broil until top is brown and dish is bubbly, about 8 minutes. Turkey slices may be substituted for chicken. Mashed potatoes go nicely with this old darling. This will serve 4.

Capitol Chicken Hash

Power breakfasts in Washington D.C. are an important part of the political process. Vital political decisions are discussed informally, friendships are made, and tidbits about the social world of the city are exchanged. Chicken hash has always been popular for this morning meal; it was a favorite of President Andrew Jackson.

3–4	cups finely cubed cooked chicken
1	cup fresh chopped mushrooms (optional)
1	diced green onion
1	cup cream
2	tablespoons fresh minced parsley
	salt and pepper to taste
	pinch of nutmeg
2	tablespoons butter
2	tablespoons vegetable oil or bacon drippings

Place first 7 ingredients in a bowl and mix together. If you have some leftover chicken gravy, it may be used instead of cream. Melt butter and oil in a frying pan until hot, but not bubbling. Add the hash mixture. Cook 4 minutes over medium-high heat. Reduce heat, cover pan, and cook an additional 10 minutes. Flop out of the pan onto a warmed platter so the browned side is facing up. This will serve 4, and goes splendidly with bacon and poached eggs!

Greenwich Village Chicken Cacciatore

Years ago, when Gordon and I moved from California to New York, I wanted to live in Greenwich Village. It sounded very bohemian and seemed the perfect spot for my art student husband and me. Unfortunately, it had been taken over by wealthy people and the rents were not affordable on our GI allowance, so we ended up living in half an apartment in Astoria. However, we could afford to dine in the village in the Italian family restaurants. On a recent visit, it was a joy to find that there was still hearty Italian fare to be found at moderate prices in colorful Greenwich Village.

1	3–4 pound chicken, cut up (or chicken parts)
½	cup flour
¼	cup olive oil
1	medium onion, chopped
2	cloves fresh garlic, minced
¼	cup red or white wine vinegar
½	teaspoon dried or fresh oregano
½	teaspoon dried fresh thyme
	salt and pepper to taste
2	cups canned whole tomatoes
1	chopped red or green bell pepper
1	cup sliced fresh mushrooms
¼	cup chopped black olives
¼	cup white wine

Coat the chicken with flour. The simplest way to do this is by the old-fashioned method of placing the flour in a paper bag, adding the chicken, and then shaking to coat with flour.

Heat oil in a large frying pan. Brown chicken on both sides (this may have to be done in two batches). Remove the chicken and add onion and garlic to the pan. Fry just until limp, then stir in wine vinegar and seasonings. Add tomatoes, breaking up any large pieces. Next, add pepper, mushrooms, olives, wine, and chicken. Cover and simmer until chicken is tender—about 45 minutes. This dish can also be baked in a 350° oven for 45 minutes. Your favorite pasta may be served with the chicken. Be sure to have some crusty Italian bread to dunk in the flavorful juices. This will serve 4–5.

Russian Tea Room Shashlik

When I first lived in New York in my youthful days, our friend Ed's father was a furrier on 57th Street. This very kind man knew that his daughter-in-law Ann and I could not afford fur coats, but he would let each of us choose a coat from his racks to borrow for the evening. This gesture transformed us from students' wives into wealthy sophisticates. Adorned in this furry attire, we loved to splurge on a special celebration at the Russian Tea Room.

There is still a magical, festive mood to this restaurant. Recently, after an absence of many years, I was here with my family to celebrate our son's inclusion in a Museum of Modern Art show. Nothing had changed. We had a party and devoured every bite of their impeccable shashlik, one of the Tea Room's most popular menu items. Faith Stewart-Gordon, the owner of the Russian Tea Room, shares her recipe here. If you're curious, it was the Tartars who introduced shashlik to Russia.

3	pounds boneless leg or shoulder of lamb
1	cup salad oil
½	cup fresh lemon juice
1	teaspoon salt
1	teaspoon freshly ground pepper
2	garlic cloves, crushed
2	large bay leaves
1½	teaspoons dried dill weed or 2 tablespoons chopped fresh dill weed
3	medium firm, ripe tomatoes, cut in halves (about 1¾ pounds)
3	medium peppers, seeded, membranes removed, cut in halves
3	small to medium onions, cut in halves

Cut all fat and gristle from the lamb. Cut the lamb into twelve 2-inch cubes. Make 2 or 3 small incisions in each lamb cube to prevent puckering during cooking. In a large bowl (do not use aluminum), combine oil, lemon juice, salt, pepper, garlic, bay leaves, and dill. Mix thoroughly. Add lamb cubes and toss with a wooden spoon to coat them evenly with the marinade. Cover and refrigerate for 8 hours or overnight, turning lamb cubes 2 or 3 times for thorough marinating. Drain and reserve marinade.

On each of six 12-inch skewers, thread 1 lamb cube, 1 tomato half, 1 pepper half, and 1 lamb cube. Arrange skewers on a large broiling rack and brush with reserved marinade. Broil about 4 inches from the heat source as follows:

5–10 minutes for rare
10–12 minutes for medium
15 minutes for well done

Turn kebabs 2 or 3 times to cook evenly, and brush frequently with the reserved marinade. At the table, slide the meat and vegetables off the skewers and onto a bed of hot cooked rice, or serve with rice pilaf.

Harlem Barbecue Sauce

When we lived in New York, some of my husband's colleagues from the Art Students League would get together for pot-luck dinners. The food contributions would be laid out on a big studio table covered with brightly colored construction paper. We ate on paper plates and everyone had a great time. One of the best dishes anyone ever brought was a platter of chicken covered with this splendid, tangy sauce.

- ½ cup butter
- 1 medium onion, minced
- 2 cloves garlic, minced
- 1 teaspoon mustard
- ½ teaspoon cayenne
- 1 teaspoon Tabasco or other hot sauce
- 2 tablespoons ketchup
- 2 tablespoons lemon juice
- 2 tablespoons red or white wine vinegar
- 1 8-ounce can tomato sauce
- 2 tablespoons finely chopped parsley
- salt and pepper to taste

Melt butter in a saucepan. Lightly cook onion and garlic just until limp (not browned). Add remaining ingredients and cook over a low flame for 10 minutes. This will make enough to "sauce" 2 chickens, 8 pork chops, or 6 pounds of spareribs, cooked as desired.

Pennsylvania Waffles

Waffle irons were a popular gift for Pennsylvania Dutch brides, who are credited with introducing waffles to our country in 1617. Thomas Jefferson enjoyed having waffle parties. He purchased his waffle irons in France and brought them home to Monticello. I have made waffles for my children's slumber parties, where they are always a popular breakfast treat.

- 2 cups flour
- 2 teaspoons baking powder
- 2 tablespoons sugar
- ½ teaspoon salt
- 2 eggs, separated
- 2 cups milk
- 6 tablespoons vegetable oil or melted butter

Combine dry ingredients and sift. Beat the egg whites until stiff and set aside. Beat egg yolks and milk together. With a whisk, beat milk and egg yolk mixture into dry ingredients until smooth. Add oil or butter. Fold in egg whites. Bake in waffle iron according to individual iron instructions. This will make 6–7 waffles. Serve with butter and syrup. South in Tennessee, creamed chicken over waffles is traditionally served for Shrove Tuesday.

Waldorf Salad

Waldorf salad is a true American classic, created for the opening of New York's Waldorf Hotel in 1893. Since then, it has come to be one of the nation's favorite salads. My mother made this salad often, and this is her version of it.

- 3 apples (red, green, or yellow)
- 3 tablespoons lemon juice
- 1 cup diced celery
- ½ cup coarsely chopped walnuts (can be lightly toasted)
- ½ cup mayonnaise
- leaves of butter or iceberg lettuce (washed)

Dice the apples. Sprinkle with lemon juice and mix for an even coating. Add remaining ingredients (except lettuce), and blend gently. Serve on lettuce leaves. This will serve 4.

There are many variations on this salad. Sometimes, a cup of cubed chicken, ham, or baby shrimp is added. For a Middle Eastern flavor, you can add 1 teaspoon curry powder and ½ cup raisins. For a Pacific feeling, try adding some pineapple chunks.

Diner Greek Salad

"Diners" are a uniquely American phenomenon. They are all over our country, and everyone knows that if you want a friendly, hearty meal, this is the place to go. The prices are most reasonable, and dinners can include an appetizer, salad, soup, main dish, and dessert, all with endless cups of coffee. One evening, we were visiting friends in Mineola, Long Island, and decided we would all go out to the local diner. The menu was extensive and I decided on a full dinner with all the trimmings. It was wonderful and filling. The owners were Greek, so of course the salad was Greek. It was beautiful to look at and even better to eat. This is the diner's recipe for Greek salad.

1	medium head of lettuce (butter lettuce works well)
1	medium cucumber
3	ripe tomatoes
10	Greek olives (Kalamata are preferred)
½	cup feta cheese, cut in small cubes
5	tablespoons olive oil
2	tablespoons lemon juice
½	teaspoon oregano
	salt and pepper to taste

Wash and cut the lettuce very finely. Place in a bowl. Peel the cucumber, leaving a few "swatches" of the green peel. Slice thinly and place on top of lettuce. Cut tomatoes in thin wedges. Place on top of cucumbers. Add the olives and feta cheese. Do not worry if the feta is not in perfect cubes, as it is a crumbly cheese. Mix oil with lemon, salt, pepper, and oregano. Pour over salad and mix gently. Serve at once. This will serve 3–4.

New York Cole Slaw

One time when our family returned to America from France, the ship we were on came into the bustling New York harbor too late in the afternoon to dock. The crew and passengers had to spend the night onboard in the port of New York. This was upsetting to some, but we were able to notify our friends to meet us the next morning and decided to enjoy this unique experience. The lights of the famed skyline slowly filled the darkening sky. Tugboats and small craft darted around in the waters. I thought of Maurice Chevalier singing "Mama, it is the port of New York." We stood on the deck and watched this animated scene with awe, and it was fun.

In the morning, we stepped down the gangplank from the big ocean liner and met our waiting friends. We all piled into their car and went to a New York City deli for pastrami sandwiches and coleslaw. It seemed the best coleslaw ever. Eastern cities all have their own variations on this salad (the name simply means "cold salad" in German). This New York version is simple and delicious.

- 1 green cabbage (2–3 pounds)
- 3 green onions, finely minced
- 1 cup mayonnaise
- 1 cup sour cream
- salt and pepper to taste
- 1 teaspoon celery seed

Quarter and core cabbage and shred very finely. Mix remaining ingredients in a bowl. Add shredded cabbage and mix well. Coleslaw is the kind of casual salad that you can feel free to add things to, such as slivered green peppers, grated carrots, sliced pineapple, etc. Add additional mayonnaise if you want a moister salad. Refrigerate for an hour to blend flavors. This may be kept in the refrigerator for up to 3 days. It will serve 4–6.

Maryann's Jersey Tomato Salad

My friend Maryann is from New Jersey. She has an Italian mother, an Irish father, and a lovely accent that is an engaging mixture of her Jersey, Irish, and Italian heritage. Maryann enjoys sharing tales of family cooking in New Jersey. One of her favorite dishes is this deceptively simple tomato salad which is a taste sensation masterpiece of Jersey summer tomatoes.

Summer in New Jersey is one of Maryann's nostalgic memories. Almost every homeowner with a little patch of green will grow lovely Jersey tomatoes. They are big, juicy, and luscious to eat right from the yard. Everyone is so proud of their August tomatoes that it is a common practice to exchange and compare tomatoes with neighbors, friends, and relatives to determine who grew the best.

> 3–4 Jersey tomatoes
> fresh basil
> extra virgin olive oil
> kosher salt
> freshly ground pepper

Quarter or eighth the tomatoes depending on the size. Place in a large mixing bowl. Sliver or tear fresh basil leaves over the tomatoes. Drizzle olive oil, salt, and pepper to taste over tomatoes. Mix very gently. Jersey tomato salad is best served at room temperature. How many this will serve depends on your appetite for tomatoes! (Fresh vine-ripened tomatoes are the nearest substitute for authentic Jersey tomatoes.)

Deli Double Chocolate Cheesecake

Every Easterner seems to have his or her very own pet delicatessen which is sort of a home away from home. I love delis because they smell so good and they always have a beautiful cake display case filled with tempting sweet sensations. At New York's Carnegie Deli, the case is motorized and slowly, slowly turns around. It is easy to become hypnotized. One of the items that is usually on display is a big chocolate cheesecake, always a crowd-pleasing dessert. If you are away from your favorite deli, try making this recipe from my friend Isabel in your home kitchen.

Chocolate Wafer Crust

1	8-ounce package chocolate wafers, finely crushed
¼	cup sugar
¼	teaspoon cinnamon
7	tablespoons melted butter

Blend wafer crumbs, sugar, cinnamon, and butter. Press crumbs in the bottom of a 9- or 10-inch springform pan and up to 3 inches around the sides. (Springform pans are a good kitchen investment. They are not costly and are certainly necessary for cheesecakes!)

Filling

2	8-ounce packages cream cheese, at room temperature
1½	cups sugar
6	tablespoons cocoa
1	teaspoon vanilla
4	eggs
4	cups (1 quart) sour cream

In a mixer, cream the cheese thoroughly; add sugar, cocoa, and vanilla, blending well. Beat in the eggs one at a time, mixing well after each addition. Add the sour cream, and mix until the filling is quite smooth.

Pour batter carefully into the crust. Bake at 350° for 1 hour and 20 minutes. The edge should be set and the middle area should look glossy. This will make 12–16 servings. For a smaller group, you can make half the recipe, baking it in a 9-inch pie pan for 30 minutes at 350°.

New York Cheesecake

Every menu in New York seems to have cheesecake among the dessert offerings. Some of these are covered with a fruit topping or a glossy sour cream frosting, some have a chocolate glaze, and some sport whipped cream whirls. This recipe is a New York classic, but of course every cook has the right to have fun with toppings! Making cheesecake is not difficult, and the taste and quality of a homemade one will amaze you.

Crust

1	stick butter (4 ounces), melted
1½	cups graham cracker crumbs (about 20 crackers)
3	tablespoons sugar
½	teaspoon cinnamon

Melt butter and blend in crumbs, sugar, and cinnamon. Press into the bottom and sides of a 9-inch springform pan. Bake at 350° for 10 minutes. Set aside to cool slightly.

Filling

3	8-ounce packages cream cheese, at room temperature
1	cup sugar
4	eggs
1	teaspoon vanilla
1	tablespoon grated lemon peel

Beat the cream cheese until smooth. Slowly add sugar until well blended. Add eggs one at a time, mixing well after each egg. Blend in vanilla and lemon peel. Carefully pour into the crust. Bake at 300° for 1 hour or until center is firm. Cool to room temperature. Frost with 1 cup sour cream mixed with 1 tablespoon sugar, or any other desired topping. Cheesecake will naturally "drop and crack" while cooling, so do not be alarmed—it is a natural process. This will serve 10–12.

Shoo-Fly Pie

How did it get this name? Most likely it is because flies were attracted to the sweetness of the molasses. When I tasted this pie in an Amish bakery in Lancaster County, I was surprised at its delicious lightness. Before I knew it, I had completely devoured a very large piece of pie and was back for a second. This pie is very popular in Pennsylvania as an accompaniment for morning coffee.

The pie is layered in the shell, with layers of crumbs alternating with layers of the molasses mixture.

1 unbaked 9-inch pie shell*

Crumb Mixture

1½ cups flour
½ cup sugar (can be part brown)
½ to 1 teaspoon cinnamon
½ teaspoon baking soda
¼ cup butter, at room temperature

Combine ingredients together in a bowl. My friend Verna, who lived in Pennsylvania for many years, recommends using your hands to rub the mixture together until it is very fine.

½ cup molasses
½ cup hot or boiling water
1 teaspoon soda
1 egg yolk

Mix the molasses and water; blend in soda and egg yolk. Pour one-third of this mixture in the pie shell, and follow with a layer of crumbs. Repeat two times. Bake at 375° for 40 minutes.

Teddy Roosevelt's Christmas Sand Tarts

Theodore Roosevelt loved to entertain guests in his Sagamore Hill home on Christmas morning. This Long Island Victorian residence is now operated by the National Park Service and is open year-round. The

---

*For basic piecrust recipe, see "Washington Apple Pie" in The Northwest and Alaska section.
 For a single crust, use one-half ingredient amounts.

grounds are spacious and the house is filled with mementos. In the kitchen is the large iron stove in which these sand tarts were freshly baked on Christmas mornings. These cookies, a favorite of Roosevelt's, are called sand tarts because the sugar and cinnamon sprinkled on top look like sand.

- ½ cup butter
- 1 cup sugar
- 2 eggs
- 1 teaspoon vanilla
- 1¾ cups flour
- 2 teaspoons baking powder
- ¼ teaspoon salt
- 4 tablespoons sugar mixed with 1 teaspoon cinnamon for topping

Place the butter in a bowl and cream it. Add sugar gradually, mixing until the mixture is light and fluffy. Add eggs, one at a time. Blend well and add vanilla. Sift the flour with baking powder and salt. Mix with first mixture. Dampen your hands and form a roll with the dough, about 1½ inches in diameter. Wrap in wax paper, and chill at least two hours or overnight.

To bake, cut slices (about ¼ inch thick) from the roll and place on a lightly greased cookie sheet. Sprinkle cookie tops with the "sand." Bake at 375° for 10–12 minutes. The cookies should be golden brown. This will make 2 dozen sand tarts.

Ann's Apple Cake

Ann and I have been friends for many decades. I first met Ann and her husband Ed on a fishing boat in Provincetown. It turned out that we both had student husbands, were on slim budgets, and had many other things in common. We four (Gordon and Ed bonded immediately as ardent fishermen) decided we would all meet at our tiny North Truro cottage to cook our catch of flounder. Their wedding anniversary was the next day, so we celebrated with more flounder and some cheap beer. After a week of flounder dinners, it was time for them to return home.

In those days of student budgets, they were living with her mom, dad, and brother on Long Island. Gordon and I planned to live in New York at the end of summer art school; Gordon was enrolled for the fall term at the Art Students League. Ann and Ed insisted we join them at the family's modest home and stay until we could find a place to live. We certainly did need their help. With all our possessions stuffed in our old Chevy's trunk, we arrived in September. Ann's mom fed us for two weeks until we finally found half an apartment in Astoria (bath in basement, bedroom, and kitchenette). During that year, we continued to have more memorable fishing trips and adventures with these dear friends. Over the past years, whenever it has been possible, we meet in California or New York. At our New York meetings, Ann always has a home-cooked dinner waiting for us. One evening it included this delicate, buttery apple cake made with those fabulous New York apples.

½ cup butter
1 cup sugar
1 beaten egg
1 cup flour
½ teaspoon baking powder
1 teaspoon cinnamon
½ teaspoon salt
3 cups diced apples (4–5 medium)
¾ cup chopped walnuts (optional)
2 tablespoons sugar mixed with 1 teaspoon cinnamon for topping

Cream butter and sugar together until light and fluffy. Add egg. Sift dry ingredients and blend. Fold in apples and walnuts. This may seem like a thick batter, but the apples will add moisture. Place in a greased and floured 9-inch springform pan. Sprinkle with the sugar and cinnamon. Bake at 350° for 1 hour. Let cool a few minutes, remove from the pan, and place on a pretty plate. This cake is delicious served with a scoop of ice cream.

Halloween Pumpkin Cupcakes

Although Halloween comes down to us from the Druids and Celts, it has evolved into one of the most popular American holidays. School festivals, door-to-door trick-or-treating, and even costume parties for adults contribute to the Halloween joviality.

Pumpkin fields can be found all around the country. New York's Long Island has many fields, which offer all the pumpkins you can carry for most reasonable prices. You will see young children struggling to hold several pumpkins and strong young men carrying big pumpkins in their muscular arms. Although pumpkins are eaten in many forms, as a vegetable and in pies, the most popular use for them is as jack-o'-lanterns, glowing spookily with a candle placed inside.

This recipe for cupcakes is a Halloween favorite. Canned pumpkin is used here, as the fresh is too runny for this version.

1	28-ounce can pumpkin
3	eggs
¾	cup vegetable oil
½	cup water
2¼	cups sugar (white or brown)
2½	cups flour
1½	teaspoons soda
¼	teaspoon salt
1	teaspoon nutmeg
1	teaspoon cinnamon
1	cup raisins

With an electric mixer, mix together in a bowl the pumpkin, eggs, oil, water, and sugar. Beat until well blended. Sift together the dry ingredients and mix into first mixture, blending until smooth. Fold in raisins. Place cupcake papers in a cupcake pan. Fill three-fourths full with batter. Bake at 350° for 45 minutes. Cool. These may be frosted but are fine just plain. The recipe will make about 2 dozen.

Mid-Atlantic Drinks

Philadelphia Winter Punch

Philadelphia has a reputation for punches. They were served in colonial days in taverns and were favorites at political gatherings. Some of the recipes from the founding of our country are very strong and create a very sweet, heady mixture. This lovely punch has replaced older recipes, and is perfect for winter parties.

- 1 quart dry white wine
- 4 oranges (any variety)
- 1 cup sugar

Slice oranges crossways and lay them in a baking pan in one layer. Bake at 300° just until they turn light brown. Remove oranges and place in a stainless steel bowl. Cover with sugar and two cups of the wine. Stir well, cover, and keep in a cool place for 24 hours. To serve, strain the mixture, pressing orange slices to release the juice. Add the remaining wine. Heat mixture in a pan. Simmer for 2 minutes. Pour into goblets (if desired, add a piece of orange rind retrieved from the strainer). This will serve 4 generously but can be easily doubled or tripled as needed.

New Jersey Egg Nog

One of the largest industries in New Jersey is poultry, so it is natural that egg nog should be popular in our Garden State. This easy variation is used every year by my New Jersey friends for holiday parties.

- 6 eggs
- 1 cup sugar
- 1 cup rum
- 1 quart cream or half-and-half
- nutmeg for topping

In a large bowl, beat the eggs until light and foamy. Add sugar, beating until thick. Chill 3 hours or more. Stir in rum and cream. Sprinkle with nutmeg. This will make 8 servings.

The Manhattan

This American cocktail was a creation of New York's Manhattan Club for a party hosted by Lady Jennie Churchill, and ever since, an air of sophistication has lingered about it.

- 2½ ounces bourbon or rye whiskey
- ½ ounce sweet vermouth
- 3 dashes Angostura bitters
- 1 maraschino cherry for garnish

Chill a 4-ounce martini-style glass. Pour whiskey, vermouth, and bitters into a mixing glass half filled with ice cubes. Stir well to blend and chill. Strain into glass and garnish with the cherry.

THE SOUTH

I grew up in California with a Southern grandmother, Lilla Wilkinson. She had been born and raised at the Myrtle Grove plantation on the Mississippi River south of New Orleans. "Nana" was a great-great-granddaughter of General James Wilkinson, who accepted the Louisiana Purchase for the United States. It is only natural that I have come to look upon the South through Nana's perspective. Her tales of Southern foods, with their mingling of exotic flavors from the Spanish, French, African, Native American, and Cajun people, sounded exciting to me. Nana was a gumbo cooking master. All her many versions of the dish were full of tantalizing flavors. When she was almost 18, she fell in love with a dashing Spanish gentleman, Fernando. Her family felt he was not the right match for her. She was sent to New York to place a distance between them. While there, she took piano lessons at the Staats Piano School, where she fell in love and married her teacher, Henry Taylor Staats. Eventually, they moved to Pasadena to begin a music school. She never returned to Louisiana but all her life continued to inspire everyone with her Southern cooking and tales of Southern life.

Because of Nana, when I visit the South I feel at home. I can visit New Orleans's Cabildo Museum and see the painting of my distant grandfather and touch the table where he signed the Louisiana Purchase. I can dine in restaurants that offer all the foods she happily cooked for me. I can visit the French Market in New Orleans to see the okra, eggplant, Creole tomatoes, sweet potatoes, peppers, garlic, peanuts, onions, and praline vendors.

It is true that New Orleans is only part of the Southern culinary heritage; however, it is the best destination for Southern dining. Flying into New Orleans, the plane will drift across the swamps. You can almost see the alligators. The taxi ride into the city passes the "above the ground" cemeteries, with their white sculptured tombs adorned with angels guarding the lifeless in these gardens of the dead. When the taxi stops at the hotel, lively music from a street saxophone player instantly puts me in the mood of the city. This is the town of eternal jazz mingled with scents of spices and chicory. Quickly, I rush out to a French Quarter restaurant where I know the menu will be filled with choices: oysters on the half shell, shrimp remoulade, gumbo soups, smoked hams, barbecued pork, catfish, crawfish étouffée, Southern drinks, flamboyant desserts, and coffee laced with chicory. These are all foods my grandmother told me about. Waiters do not rush. They call me "honey," and when several of us are dining it is "y'all," said with all the manners and hospitality of gentlemen or gentle ladies. I know I am in my Nana's South.

I have drifted up the Mississippi on the historic Delta Queen riverboat to visit the great restored Southern mansions, and I have listened to tales of this great river. A friend of ours nearly drowned in the river while out in a pirogue. A waiter at Arnaud's told me how he would swim "naked as a worm" in this muddy river with his neighborhood friends; another sailed the entire river in a tiny boat. I have been in Cajun country and have tasted alligator and spicy Cajun sausage and have heard the rhythmic music and Evangeline legends. In the perfectly restored town of Williamsburg, I have tasted peanut soup, biscuits, and colonial game pie. In our nation's proud capital, with its spacious tree-lined streets and bountiful flower beds, I have tasted fresh Virginia spring asparagus, Baltimore crab cakes, and briny Chesapeake Bay oysters in historic inns. At the farthest point of the South, in Florida, I have dined on the famed key lime pie and treasures from the tropical sea. The riches of the food of the South are among the most appealing in the nation, reflecting the influences of settlers, immigrants, and gentry.

The South is deeply imbued with our nation's history. On the Gettysburg battlefields, the famous battle is relived and reconstructed by avid Civil War buffs. In Richmond, kindly ladies will show you where Patrick Henry stood and the grave of Edgar Allen Poe's mother. A senior docent in the Virginia State capitol claims that the statue of Robert E. Lee winks at her as she finishes her tour duties. Ladies of eight decades will lead you up and down stairways and long hallways in Southern historic houses. During special Southern pilgrimages, family members dressed in antique Southern attire will guide you around their gardens and offer refreshments on antique bone china. The hospitality is warm and plentiful.

The Southern states are blessed with a rich, fertile soil and a tropical climate that produces exotic fruits, rice, chicory, sweet potatoes, and peanuts. Wild game and fish fill the forests and waters. The mysterious swamps have offered them a refuge from persecution and a natural preserve. The scenery is ravishing, with multitudes of meandering plants and Spanish moss draping over the trees. The dramatic weather includes torrential rains, high humidity, hurricanes, and intense summer heat.

When I was about 10, I read the Southern saga *Gone With the Wind*. My mother and Nana had a lengthy discussion about whether it was proper reading for my age. With my persuasion, they gave in and I was completely engrossed in it for several days. I must freely admit that this stirring novel added to my fascination with the South. I like to reflect on the strong character of Scarlett O' Hara and her love of fine Southern food: "As God is my witness, I'm never going to be hungry again!" Southern cooks continue to take very great pride in a heritage of cooking that began with the colonists' first campfire in Virginia.

Shrimp Remoulade

This delectable appetizer makes a perfect beginning to any dinner. Fresh Gulf shrimp are firm and full of sea flavor. My Southern grandmother preferred to use pretty little glass dishes to serve remoulade, and I still think this is the nicest way to do it. In the South, however, you may also find remoulade served on little saucers or even in tiny bowls.

- 3 cups cooked shrimp, peeled and deveined (approximately ¾ pound)
- 3 cups finely shredded iceberg lettuce

Remoulade Sauce

- ⅔ cup ketchup
- ½ teaspoon dry mustard (or prepared)
- 2 tablespoons horseradish
- ½ teaspoon hot pepper sauce or Tabasco
- 1 tablespoon minced green onions
- 1 tablespoon minced parsley

Combine the shrimp with the blended sauce ingredients, and chill. When ready to serve, finely shred the lettuce and divide into 6 portions. Carefully spoon the shrimp on top of the lettuce.

Virginia Peanut Soup

Peanuts are a significant crop in the South. They originated in South America and were introduced into Africa as a payment for slaves. In turn, slaves brought the peanut into the South. Originally it was thought of as a food for livestock and the poor, but after starving Civil War soldiers ate peanuts to survive, its popularity increased. Today, Americans consume 800 million pounds of peanuts a year. There is the same amount of protein in a pound of peanuts as in an equal amount of beef. One of the joys of Southern travel is a visit to Monticello where our

Southern president, Thomas Jefferson, grew peanuts among his many other crops. His carefully kept garden journals are on display.

This pleasant soup is served in the charming historic restaurants of Williamsburg and is popular in many Southern states.

- 1 tablespoon butter
- 1 small onion, finely chopped (about ⅓ cup)
- 1 tablespoon flour
- 4 cups chicken broth
- 2 cups smooth peanut butter
- salt and pepper to taste
- 1 teaspoon celery salt (optional)
- ½ cup half-and-half
- 1 cup chopped peanuts for topping
- chives or parsley for topping

In a soup pot, melt the butter, add the onion, and stir-fry just until limp. Blend in the flour. Gradually add the chicken broth, stirring until smooth. Blend in the peanut butter. Stirring with a fork or whisk will help in this blending. Cook over a very low flame for 20 minutes, stirring occasionally. Taste for seasoning, adding celery salt if desired. Add the half-and-half, stir, and serve at once. Garnish with nuts and chives or parsley. This will serve 5, and may be served hot or cold.

Thomas Jefferson Deviled Crab

This renaissance president was a native of Virginia and had a special fondness for such Southern foods as deviled crab. Jefferson loved wine and entertaining. At the end of his first year in the White House, his entertainment expenses were over $12,000—more than the presidential income. Of course, because he was an impeccable president, it was paid for out of his personal funds.

If you do not live near a good source for fresh crab, frozen may be substituted. A glass of cool dry white wine served with this delicious dish adds a nice touch.

1	pound fresh crab meat (imitation crab may be used)
¼	cup butter
1	medium red pepper, chopped
4	green onions, minced
1	tablespoon flour
2	cups half-and-half
¼	teaspoon cayenne
1	tablespoon Dijon-style mustard
2	tablespoons brandy or white wine
¼	cup bread crumbs
	minced parsley for garnish

Melt the butter in a heavy saucepan. Add the pepper and onion. Fry over a low flame just until limp. Add the flour to the pan and blend well. Next, add the half-and-half, cayenne, and mustard. Stir over low flame until the mixture is slightly thick. Add liquor and crab meat.

Place in a buttered baking dish or 4 individual dishes or baking shells. Sprinkle the bread crumbs on top and bake at 350° for 20 minutes. Garnish with minced parsley. This will serve 4.

Shrimp Jambalaya

The renowned American folk singer Hank Williams relished singing the song "Jambalaya." This music makes eating jambalaya on the bayou sound like so much fun, and it *is* fun both to prepare and to devour this typical Southern dish. The name is part French and part African. *Jambon* is French for ham, and *la ya* is rice in an African dialect. Some recipe versions include sausage, oysters, or crabs, but the original recipes simply use ham, rice, and shrimp.

½	pound medium shrimp, peeled and deveined
1	cup diced ham
2	tablespoons butter or bacon drippings
1	clove garlic, minced
2	medium onions, chopped
1	green or red pepper, chopped
¼	cup diced celery
1	cup raw rice
½	teaspoon thyme, fresh or dried
¼ to ½	teaspoon cayenne
	salt and pepper to taste
1	16-ounce can solid pack or diced tomatoes (2 cups)
3	cups liquid (can be mixture of white wine, stock, and water)

In a heavy casserole (3-quart or close), melt the butter or drippings. Lightly brown garlic, onion, pepper, and celery. Add the rice and ham. Stir-fry the mixture for a minute until the rice is glossy looking.

Add the seasonings, shrimp, and tomatoes (including the liquid in the can). Add remaining liquid. Cover with a tight lid. Cook 25–30 minutes over low heat, stirring gently once or twice during cooking. The jambalaya is done when the liquid is absorbed but mixture is still moist. This will serve 6.

Myrtle Grove Plantation Gumbo

"Nana" was my grandmother on my mother's side of our family. Because I was her first grandchild, I was special to her; we had a lot in common and were very close. I was the perfect audience for her tales of plantation life at Myrtle Grove. In the early mornings, shrimp sellers would come to the plantation, offering the finest Gulf shrimp. There were chickens in the barnyard and ham in the smokehouse. Okra grew in the plantation gardens. These ingredients were all combined for the delicious plantation gumbo. The Wilkinsons always had large bowls of hot rice to accompany this dish.

My husband and I lived in an apartment in Hermosa Beach next to Nana the first years we were married. She had designed this Hermosa Beach apartment with long Southern-style hallways to spend summers away from her hot Pasadena home. When we would come home from school and work, Nana often had gumbo waiting for our dinner. It tasted wonderful, as Nana was a gumbo master.

Recently, when we visited New Orleans, a friend drove us down the Mississippi road to see if the Myrtle Grove plantation was still standing. Alas, a hurricane had blown it away decades ago. Luckily, I was able to find an old photo of it. Myrtle Grove really did look like my childhood dream fantasy of Tara in *Gone With the Wind*.

With the growing popularity and availability of Louisiana sausage, you may wish to use this in place of the ham. Gumbo is a perfect party dish, and if made a day ahead, the flavors will mellow beautifully.

¼	cup oil to fry the chicken in
1	chicken (about 3 pounds), cut up
1	cup diced ham (Tasso, if available)
1	large onion, chopped
	salt and pepper to taste
2	tablespoons parsley
1	28-ounce can solid pack tomatoes
1	cup white wine (optional)
3	cups okra, sliced (fresh, frozen, or canned)
1	pound medium shrimp, peeled and deveined

In a large frying pan, fry the chicken pieces, ham, and onion until lightly browned. This procedure is a sort of light stir-fry to give a toasty flavor and seal in the chicken juices. Remove to a large soup pot or Dutch oven. Add salt, pepper, parsley, and tomatoes, cutting up any large pieces of tomato. If you wish, 1 cup of white wine can be added for extra zest. The liquid should just cover the chicken; if it seems low, add extra water. Cover and simmer until the chicken is tender, about 50 minutes.

Remove chicken and cool until it is easy to handle. Remove meat from the bones, cutting into bite-sized pieces. Return chicken meat to the pot. Cut okra in ½-inch slices; add okra and shrimp to chicken mixture and cook uncovered for about 10 minutes. My Nana did not use filé powder, as she felt the okra was enough thickening. Serve to 6 with generous portions of steamed rice.

Southern Fried Chicken with Cream Gravy

Southern fried chicken is enjoyed by people all over the United States. It is as American as apple pie! Of course, there is fabulous fried chicken and some that is not so fabulous. There are a few secrets.

First, the chicken should be a fryer from 2½ to 3 pounds, cut nicely into 2 thighs, 2 drumsticks, 2 breasts, and 2 wings. Marinating in buttermilk adds flavor. If desired, chicken parts may also be used. The medium you use to fry the chicken is very important. Lard is the best, followed by oil and shortening. An iron frying pan is a must. This is somewhat of a messy job but well worth the effort.

Please do not be alarmed about frying food. When you fry it correctly, the flavors are sealed inside. Fried foods are placed for a minute on paper towels to remove any excess fat. The good news is that the latest studies show that lard is a natural product and not at all the culprit it has been made out to be. All of our grandmothers used lard, and they certainly were sturdy survivors.

- 1 chicken (2½–3 pounds), cut up, or parts
- 1 cup buttermilk (just enough to cover chicken)
- 1 cup flour
- salt and pepper to taste
- 1 teaspoon paprika
- 1 teaspoon cayenne (optional)
- lard, shortening, or oil for frying—enough to make 1-inch depth

Cream Gravy

- 3 tablespoons pan drippings
- 3 tablespoons flour
- 1½ cups milk or buttermilk
- salt and pepper to taste

Place the chicken pieces in a bowl. Cover with the buttermilk and stir around so all pieces are coated. Cover and refrigerate for at least an hour;

even overnight is fine. In a paper bag, combine the dry ingredients. Remove the chicken from the buttermilk and slightly drain. Place pieces in the bag and shake to coat with flour mixture. Heat the frying medium in a frying pan until it sizzles when you place a bread cube in the pan. Place the chicken in the pan with tongs (forks break the skin). Do not crowd; you may need two iron frying pans. Cover and cook 15 minutes at medium heat. Turn chicken and fry an additional 15–20 minutes.

Place the chicken pieces on a platter lined with paper towels and put in a 200° oven while you make the cream gravy. Pour off frying medium to leave 3 tablespoons in the pan. Add flour, and over low heat stir to incorporate any bits left in the pan. Slowly add milk or buttermilk. Stir until mixture is thick and smooth. Season with salt and pepper to taste. Serve over rice or mashed potatoes with the delicious fried chicken. This will serve 4.

Brunswick Stew

Brunswick stew is the subject of intense rivalry in a real Southern stew war. Brunswick County, North Carolina, has issued a proprietary claim. The coastal city of Brunswick, Georgia, claims the stew belongs to them; and then there is Brunswick County, Georgia, also claiming it originated there. These stew wars are carried on in the joyous form of Brunswick stew festivals. The tasty mixture is prepared in huge cauldrons (one of them a 25-gallon cast-iron pot) and is stirred with giant wooden paddles.

What is Brunswick stew? One of the legends suggests that it originated when a camp cook for Dr. Creed Haskins' Virginia hunting party prepared a blend of local squirrel, bacon, onions, and stale bread for the hungry returning hunters. Today, chicken has, for the most part, replaced squirrel, and different cooks have their own special recipes.

Dr. Haskins discovered, when he became a member of the House of Delegates, that Brunswick stew added a special conviviality to political gatherings with friends. The stew continues to be served at fundraisers in the South. This dish is perfect for large parties and may be served with cornbread and coleslaw. A romantically Southern pastime is to cook Brunswick stew over a hickory-log fire in the woods on a moonlit night.

3	pounds chicken (parts or whole chicken)
2	quarts water (2 cups may be white wine)
2	medium onions, chopped
2	cups diced canned or fresh tomatoes
	salt and pepper to taste
3	medium potatoes, peeled and chopped (1½ to 2 cups)
2	cups fresh, frozen, or canned corn
1	10-ounce package frozen lima beans

Place chicken in a stew pot. Cover with water; add onions, tomatoes, salt, and pepper. Cover and simmer until tender, about 1 hour. Remove chicken from broth, cool, and remove meat. Cut into small bite-sized pieces. While you are preparing the chicken, cook the potatoes in the broth for about twenty minutes. When potatoes are tender, add the chicken, lima beans, and corn and continue to simmer for another 30 minutes. Serve to 6 in soup bowls. Like all stews, this one is even better the next day.

Pulled Pork Sandwiches

"Pulled pork" sandwiches are the all-around darling of the South's sandwich world. One of the best I ever tasted was in the historic city of Harper's Ferry, where the little hillside cafes that line the meandering road to the river offer cool beer with these tasty sandwiches. The secret is a fresh and sturdy bun filled with just the right amount of that smoky tender pork. Pulled pork is simply a piece of pork cooked so long (either in the oven or barbecue) that it is so tender it can be pulled into shreds. It can be a great summer party dish.

1	pork shoulder roast (5–6 pounds)
⅓	cup Wright's or other liquid smoke
	salt and pepper

THE SOUTH

Sauce

2	minced garlic cloves
	salt and pepper to taste
	pan juices
4	cups ketchup
2	tablespoons Tabasco or other hot sauce
	hamburger buns or other style rolls for the sandwiches

The meat can be barbecued in a smoker until well done, cooled, and shredded. A quicker, easier method is to score the meat on both sides to a ½-inch depth and rub with liquid smoke, salt, and pepper. Wrap with double foil and bake for 4 hours in a 325° oven, on a rack set in a baking pan. Cool and shred. Mix sauce ingredients together with pork. This may be done ahead and the mixture warmed before serving, in a casserole in the oven. Set the casserole on the table and serve buffet-style with a basket of buns.

Hoppin' John

There is a passage in Tennessee Williams's "Cat on a Hot Tin Roof" in which Big Mama is encouraged about the health of Big Daddy because he has eaten two portions of Hoppin' John. Southern legends say that Hoppin' John was a lame plantation cook who hopped on one leg while serving this dish. If leftovers are served, they are called "skipping Jenny," after his wife who skipped. In some Southern households, children like to get into a playful game of hopping once around the table before they sit down to eat. This is a large recipe, making plenty for big daddies. It freezes well and is a good leftover.

1	pound dried black-eyed peas
1	onion, peeled and chopped
½	pound bacon slices
	salt and pepper to taste
2	cups long-grain rice

Place the peas and chopped onion in a large deep heavy pot. Cover with water. You will need enough water for the peas to expand. Add the bacon, and season with salt and pepper. Cover and simmer until barely tender, about 1 hour.

Uncover and add more water, if needed; you will need 4 cups of liquid to cook the rice. Add rice and simmer covered for about 30 minutes. The rice and peas should not be mushy. Each serving should have a slice of bacon. Serve with hot sauce if desired. This makes about 6 servings.

Red Beans and Rice

America's favorite trumpeter, Louis Armstrong, used to complain to his fellow musicians that when they were on the road it was impossible for him to find any good Louisiana red beans and rice. Traditionally, this is a Louisiana Monday dish using the ham bone from Sunday dinner. However, it is so popular that it certainly can be found on Southern menus any day.

- 1 pound dried red or kidney beans
- 1 small ham hock, or a ham bone with some meat, or ¼ pound salt pork (diced)
- 1 onion, chopped
- 1 clove garlic, minced
- salt and pepper to taste
- pinch of cayenne (optional)
- chopped green onions for garnish
- hot cooked rice (about 6 cups)

Cover beans with fresh water, about 6 cups. The water should come to about 2–3 inches above the beans. Add remaining ingredients. Simmer until the beans are tender, but not mushy. This will take about 1½ hours. Remove the ham hock or bone and cut the ham in small pieces. Return ham to pot.

This is served in bowls on top of hot cooked rice. Sometimes the rice. is added to the pot and mixed with the beans. Garnish with chopped green onions. Serve with a fresh green salad and some good bread to wipe the bowls clean. This will serve 6.

Fourth of July Macaroni and Cheese

Happy picnics are part of our Fourth of July celebrations. My mother liked to include macaroni and cheese in her holiday menu. This is a popular dish and was a favorite of president Thomas Jefferson, who brought a recipe for preparing macaroni from France. Making this dish carefully was important to my mother. She cooked the macaroni just to the perfect, barely tender stage and used premium sharp cheddar cheese. It was baked in a pretty casserole and served piping hot.

½	pound elbow macaroni
4	tablespoons butter
4	tablespoons flour
2	cups milk
1	green onion, minced
	salt and pepper to taste
2	cups grated sharp cheddar cheese
2	tablespoons bread crumbs
	parsley and paprika for garnish

Cook the macaroni in rapidly boiling salted water until tender but not mushy. Drain and set aside while you make the sauce. Melt the butter in a heavy saucepan. Add the flour. Blend well and cook together for a minute. Stir in the milk, onion, salt, and pepper. Cook over a low flame, stirring to make a smooth mixture. Blend in the grated cheese as the sauce is cooking. When the sauce has thickened, mix with the macaroni. Place in a buttered 2- to 3-quart attractive baking dish and sprinkle the bread crumbs over the top. Bake at 350° for 20–25 minutes until bubbly and light brown on top.

This dish can be prepared ahead and refrigerated if desired; add an extra 15–20 minutes for baking. This will serve 4.

Baked Virginia Cheese Grits

Visitors to the South like to joke about grits, a staple served at breakfast, lunch, and dinner. Grits are simply coarsely ground dried corn kernels with a few seasonings. Many servicemen who were stationed in the South may have memories of unattractive mess-hall grits, but when grits are properly prepared (which is simple), they are most satisfying and pleasant. They can be turned into a lovely side dish to accompany any food. Southern chefs these days are having fun adding mushrooms, turnip greens, or cheeses to their grits. This recipe is a popular one.

- ¾ cup quick-cooking grits
- 3 cups water
- ½ teaspoon salt
- 1 cup milk
- 1 egg, beaten
- 4 green onion tops, thinly sliced crossways
- 1½ cups grated cheddar cheese
- 1 teaspoon hot pepper sauce (optional)
- 2 tablespoons butter, at room temperature

Heat water and salt to boiling. Slowly stir in the grits. Cover pan and cook over low heat for 6 minutes, stirring now and then so grits do not stick to pan. Mix remaining ingredients. Remove grits from pan and blend well with this mixture. Place all in a greased 1½- or 2-quart baking dish, and bake uncovered at 350° for 20 minutes. This will serve 4.

Skillet Cornbread

Cornbread is deeply embedded in American culinary culture. The corn provided by Native Americans did indeed save early settlers from starvation. In the South, even after wheat flour became a crop and alternative for bread, corn remained the favorite.

Iron skillets are part of a Southern bride's dowry, and the secret to the South's fabulous cornbread is the use of these skillets. Every kitchen has a favorite cornbread recipe. The pan with shortening is preheated in the oven. When the batter is placed in the pan there will be a sizzling noise. This hot "searing" of the batter is what creates the fabulous crust.

- 1 cup flour
- 4 teaspoons baking powder
- 4 tablespoons sugar
- 1 teaspoon salt
- 1 cup yellow or white cornmeal
- 2 eggs, beaten
- 1 cup milk or buttermilk
- ¼ cup melted butter, oil, bacon drippings, or shortening, plus 2 tablespoons extra for bottom of pan

Sift dry ingredients (except cornmeal). Blend in cornmeal with a fork. In a separate bowl, mix eggs, milk, and melted (slightly cooled) shortening with a whisk or fork. Add the liquid to the dry ingredients. Stir together with a spoon, but do not overmix. Heat a 9- or 10-inch iron skillet with 2 tablespoons of the butter, oil, drippings, or shortening in a preheated 425° oven for 7 minutes. Remove from oven. Place the batter in the pan and return to bake at 425° for 20–25 minutes. Cut in wedges and serve from the skillet. This will serve 6.

Kentucky Scramble

Leisurely breakfasts are a way of life in Kentucky. This splendid combination of corn and peppers folded in with scrambled eggs is delightful to look at and even better to feast upon. It goes very well with some potatoes and fresh cornbread. Mint juleps are the favored drink for breakfast or any time of a Kentucky day.

8	lean slices bacon
1	cup corn kernels, preferably fresh, or canned or frozen
1	medium green pepper, finely chopped
¼	cup finely chopped pimiento or red pepper
3	green onion tops, finely sliced
10	eggs
	salt and pepper to taste
½	teaspoon Tabasco or other red pepper sauce (optional)

Cook bacon in a large skillet until crisp. Remove and place on paper towels to absorb fat. Add the vegetables to the drippings remaining in the pan and cook uncovered over medium heat until wilted, about 5 minutes. With a whisk, beat the eggs together with salt and pepper (and hot sauce, if used). Add to vegetable mixture. Stir over low heat until eggs are set but still creamy. Divide into six portions on warmed plates. Crumble the bacon and garnish each portion with the bacon crumbles. This will serve 6.

Eggs Sardou

Eggs Sardou was created decades ago by Antoine, owner of the renowned New Orleans restaurant, for a special dinner he hosted for the French playwright Victorien Sardou. Today in New Orleans, this is popular as a featured brunch entrée. There are many variations of it, with additions of everything from anchovy fillets to truffle slices.

Breakfast at Brennan's is always a must when visiting the Crescent City. Sitting in the restaurant's bricked patio amidst green plants, enjoying a superbly prepared order of Eggs Sardou with a glass of champagne, certainly will be a special memory of your visit. If you prepare this dish at home, you most likely will want to use one of the simple versions, such as this one.

1	cup hot creamed spinach (made with fresh or frozen spinach and ¼ cup cream or cream cheese)
2	artichoke hearts
1	tablespoon butter
2	poached eggs
½	cup prepared Hollandaise sauce (canned, or dry mix), heated*

Fresh or frozen spinach may be used. If using fresh, you will need 1 bunch. Wash well. Cook over a low flame for 5 minutes in just enough salted water to cling to the leaves. Drain and chop. If using frozen, buy the kind that's already chopped and follow package directions. Drain well and mix with cream or cream cheese. Set aside.

Lightly warm the artichoke hearts in the butter. (Artichoke hearts are found frozen or in cans, or can be taken from fresh artichokes if you have the time.) Poach eggs in a poacher or by dropping in hot boiling water to which 2 tablespoons vinegar has been added and simmering for 4 minutes.

Warm two plates. Place an artichoke heart on each plate. Carefully lay the spinach on the heart, making a little nest. Set the eggs in the nest. Dribble the Hollandaise sauce over the eggs and serve immediately. This will serve one or two, depending on your appetite.

Pelican Club Mashed Sweet Potatoes

The handsome Pelican Club is one of the most celebrated dining spots in New Orleans. The menu is full of fantastic food combinations, all with a very Southern influence. Under the creative and attentive talent of Louisiana-born chef Richard Hughes, Jr., each dish arrives at your table as a personal kitchen masterpiece. On one city visit, I went back three times just to taste again the braised hickory-smoked duckling, which is served with a wild rice, cashew, and raisin combination and a side of the restaurant's own famous mashed sweet potatoes. The

---

*For easy homemade Hollandaise sauce, see recipe under "New York Chicken Divan" in The Middle Atlantic section.

most amicable and charming Chef Hughes is happy to share his recipe for this popular dish.

5	pounds sweet potatoes
½	cup light brown sugar
¾	pound cold butter
1	teaspoon salt
1	ounce vanilla
¼	teaspoon cayenne pepper
1	teaspoon cinnamon
	juice of 1 lemon
½	cup orange juice

Wash the sweet potatoes but do not peel them. Place in a pot, cover with water and 1 teaspoon salt, and cook over medium flame until tender (about 35 minutes). Drain potatoes, peel, and whip in mixer, gradually adding remaining ingredients until everything is well blended and potatoes are light in consistency. Correct seasonings, if necessary, and keep warm. This serves 16, but can easily be halved to serve 8.

Delta Queen Bread Pudding

To drift down the Mississippi on the Delta Queen steamboat is an incomparable adventure. The Queen is the smallest of the Delta fleet, and because of this the trip seems like a leisurely cruise with intimate friends. The ship pulls up to the riverbanks (a rope is just latched around a tree) of historic American towns, where fascinating shore trips are offered. During the time of my cruise there were Spring Pilgrimage days in Natchez, during which the owners of beautiful and graceful Southern properties greeted us and proudly showed their historic homes. Tables were set with precious family china and silver, and bouquets of azaleas and camellias filled the rooms.

Delicious food is served in the Queen's vintage dining room. There are samples of Southern food every day: collard greens, grits, gumbo, jambalaya, and sumptuous desserts, including this bread pudding which is one of my favorites. The sous-chef Mr. Huff shared his recipe for it, which is presented here in a smaller-sized version for home use.

1	large loaf good-quality white bread (can be day old)
1	cup pecan pieces
¾	cup raisins
3	eggs
2½	cups milk
1½	cups sugar
1	tablespoon cinnamon
3	tablespoons vanilla
⅛	cup butter, melted

Cut bread into 2-inch cubes to make about 5 cups and place in a large mixing bowl. Add pecans and raisins. Mix eggs, milk, sugar, cinnamon, vanilla, and melted butter together until well blended. Pour over the bread and allow it to soak up the mixture (about 30 minutes). Pour into a well-buttered 2-quart baking pan. Bake at 350° for 40 to 45 minutes until golden brown and the center springs up when pushed down. Serve warm with whiskey sauce.

Whiskey Sauce

1	cup butter
1	cup brown sugar
3	tablespoons whiskey

Melt butter, blend in sugar, and cook together 3 minutes. Add whiskey and cook an additional minute. Serve hot on top of pudding. This will make 6 servings.

Brennan's Bananas Foster

High on almost every New Orleans visitor's list is breakfast at Brennan's, which truly is a fantastic and memorable experience. Inside the entrance from busy Royal Street, a lovely patio oasis of exotic plants, cooled by breezes from the palmetto fans, helps to create a tropical mood. The Brennan family are the master restaurateurs of the Crescent City. With true Southern generosity, they offered to share this recipe.

The classic breakfast will include oyster soup Brennan and a delectable egg dish (Eggs Sardou or Eggs Hussarde, a Brennan's original), and will end with the theatrical presentation of Bananas Foster prepared at your table. Brennan's chef Paul created this dish in 1951 and named it for Richard Foster, a special friend of Owen Brennan. It is the most requested item at Brennan's, where each year 35,000 pounds of bananas are used in preparing this dish.

- ¼ cup (½ stick) butter
- 1 cup brown sugar
- ½ teaspoon cinnamon
- ¼ cup banana liqueur
- 4 bananas, cut in half lengthwise, then halved
- ¼ cup dark rum
- 4 scoops vanilla ice cream

Combine butter, sugar, and cinnamon in a flambé pan or skillet. Place the pan over low heat and cook, stirring, until sugar dissolves. Stir in the banana liqueur, then place the bananas in the pan. When the bananas soften and begin to brown, carefully add the rum. Continue to cook the sauce until the rum is hot, then tip the pan slightly and ignite the rum. When the flames subside, lift the bananas out of the pan. Place four pieces over each portion of ice cream. Generously spoon warm sauce over the top and serve immediately. This will serve 4.

Key Lime Pie

Early Spanish settlers brought the lime to Florida. The lime trees adapted quickly to the climate of the Florida Keys and have flourished there. These "key limes" were the variety that the British Navy used to protect its sailors from scurvy, which earned their sailors the nickname "limeys." They drank the lime juice with rum to make the cure more palatable.

As with any popular American pie, there are many versions of this one. Some are sickly sweet or artificially colored a weird green. My neighbor's sister lives in Florida and offered this excellent recipe, which has the perfect flavor balance.

Graham Cracker Crust

18	single graham crackers
¼	cup melted butter
2	tablespoons sugar
	dash of cinnamon and nutmeg

Crush the crackers into fine crumbs (I put them in a plastic bag and whack them with a rolling pin). Combine with the butter, sugar, and spices. Mix with your hands or a spoon and pat into an 8- or 9-inch pie pan. Bake at 350° for 8 minutes, then set aside to cool.

Pie Filling

1	14-ounce can sweetened condensed milk
3	eggs (separated)
3	limes
1	cup whipping cream

Mix the milk and beaten egg yolks. Squeeze the limes. Add juice to milk mixture. Whip the egg whites until stiff. Fold into milk mixture. Spoon into pie shell. Bake at 250° for 10 minutes. When cool, place in the refrigerator.

To serve, whip cream and spread on top of the pie. A little sugar and rum may be added to the cream if desired. This makes 6 servings.

Savannah Pumpkin Pecan Pie

The city of Savannah is a popular destination for many tourists today. This charming and historic Southern city is alluring. It has come a long way since the first settlement of colonists arrived from a debtors' prison in England. The British government hoped they would help protect the new colony from the Spaniards and natives. This pie is a Georgia Thanksgiving favorite. The word "pecan" derives from the Cree word *pagan*, referring to a hard-shelled nut. Georgia is the leading producer of pecans.

Graham Cracker Crust

- ½ cup melted butter
- 1½ cups graham cracker crumbs
- 3 tablespoons confectioners sugar
- ½ teaspoon cinnamon
- ¼ teaspoon nutmeg

Melt the butter. Blend with remaining ingredients. Press into a 9-inch pie pan. Chill one hour before filling.

Pie Filling

- 1 quart vanilla ice cream (slightly softened)
- ½ cup brown sugar
- 1 cup canned pumpkin (or 1 cup fresh, cooked and mashed)
- 1 teaspoon cinnamon
- ½ teaspoon nutmeg
- 1 tablespoon brandy (optional)
- ¼ teaspoon salt

Topping

- 1 cup whipping cream
- ½ cup toasted chopped pecans

Place the ice cream in a bowl. Add the brown sugar, pumpkin, spices, and brandy if used. Blend together. Gently place in the pie shell and freeze for at least 6 hours. For make-ahead convenience, it can stay in the freezer for up to a week.

To serve: Whip the cream, spread on top of the pie, and sprinkle the pecans over the top. This will serve 6–8.

Ambrosia

A Southern Christmas table always includes ambrosia. In some states, this cool and lovely Southern dessert has suffered from the attention of cooks who add ingredients that do not belong, such as miniature marshmallows and sour cream. This simple, pristine dish should be made in true Southern fashion, as follows.

8	medium oranges
1	cup sugar
1½	cups grated coconut (can be packaged, but fresh is best)
½	cup dry sherry

Peel the oranges and cut into thin slices (remove seeds). Mix gently with sugar. Place a layer of oranges, followed by a layer of coconut, in a pretty glass bowl. Repeat layers until ingredients are used up. Pour the sherry over all and give a tiny stir just to make sure the sherry penetrates the ambrosia. Cover with foil or plastic wrap and chill about an hour before serving. This will serve 6.

Cooling Southern Drinks

Cooling drinks are part of the South. Where temperatures and humidity reach over 100 degrees and 100 percent, liquids are vital. Restaurants in the South always automatically offer water. The New Orleans restaurant Commander's Palace serves water full of crushed ice, almost a snow-cone. Iced tea and lemonade are widely served thirst-quenchers, along with Dixie beer, fine Southern bourbons, varied coffee concoctions, and powerful mixed stimulants. These are a few of the popular favorites.

Mint Julep

To hold a frosted silver cup in your hand and find your senses aroused by this mint and bourbon melange certainly makes for a rhapsodic moment. Mint juleps are traditionally served at the Kentucky Derby and Churchill Downs.

For each drink you will need:

- 6 tender fresh mint leaves
- 1 tablespoon confectioners sugar
- 1 tablespoon cold water
-   crushed ice
- 4 ounces Kentucky bourbon

If you do not own a silver mint julep cup, you may use any 8-ounce cup. Place the mint, sugar, and water in the cup. Using a bar muddler or wooden spoon, gently crush the mint. Stir until sugar dissolves. Add crushed ice, and then the bourbon. Stir with a long-handled spoon. Place in the refrigerator for 20 minutes for the glass to frost. Serve with a long straw and a sprig of mint on top. Hold the glass with a cocktail napkin when serving it so your hand will not disturb the frost.

Sazerac

New Orleans has the honor of being the birthplace of America's first cocktail. In 1790, Antoine Peychaud, a French refugee, had an apothecary shop on Royal Street. Antoine concocted a blend of bitters and brandy in a French egg cup called a *coquetier,* and somehow a curious interpretation has turned this word into "cocktail." After the Civil War, whiskey was used instead of brandy.

- 1 jigger bourbon whiskey
- 2 dashes anisette
-   dash of Pernod
-   dash of Angostura bitters
-   cherry for garnish

Shake with cracked ice and strain into cocktail glass. Garnish with a cherry.

Ramos Gin Fizz

Mr. Henry Ramos, a colorful New Orleans bartender, invented this combination which is shaken most dramatically. For the 1915 Mardi Gras, 35 boys were hired at his bar to keep up with all the shaking. This cool and refreshing drink is the popular choice for New Orleans jazz brunches.

	juice of ½ lime
	juice of ½ lemon
1	tablespoon sweet cream
	white of 1 egg
1	tablespoon granulated sugar
2	ounces dry gin
	cracked ice
	club soda

Combine all ingredients except club soda in a shaker, and shake vigorously until foamy. The boys at Ramos' do this for 10 minutes! Strain into a 10-ounce glass and add a splash of club soda.

Cajun Coffee

This is an old Cajun combination that combines two of the South's special flavorings—molasses and coffee. It is a pleasant accompaniment to dessert.

3	cups strong black coffee
¼	cup molasses
1	cup cream, whipped
	dash of nutmeg
	rum (optional)

Mix coffee and molasses and heat to a low simmer. Stir to blend. Divide mixture between 4 cups or heat-proof glasses. Top with cream and a dash of nutmeg. The idea is to sip the coffee mixture through the cream, much like Irish coffee. Some Cajuns like to mix a tablespoon of rum in with the coffee and molasses. This will serve 4.

Southern Summer Lemonade

Driving around Southern roads in the summer in an air-conditioned car can be a comfortable enough experience. However, the minute you open the door and step out into the real weather, it is sort of like a hot blast furnace exploding all over you. As you are driving, you will see people sitting in chairs on their spacious front porches with portable fans, drinking lemonade. This is a way to keep cool and relaxed. Lemonade is very much an American drink and one of our finest. Of course, you can simply buy a can of frozen concentrated lemonade, but it will never compare with the taste of freshly made.

- 2 fresh lemons (for about ⅓ cup juice)
- ¾ cup sugar
- 1 quart water
- sprigs of mint
- ice cubes

Squeeze lemons; add sugar, water, and mint. Shake well and refrigerate for flavors to mellow (½ to 6 hours). Pour over ice cubes and serve. This will make 4 large glasses. If desired, a few strips of peel may be added at the beginning for a more intense flavor.

THE HEARTLAND

The Heartland is the vast center of our country. It is a land of fertile plains, deep woods, lakes, orchards, and miles of dairy land. Small towns dot the landscape and are surrounded by farms, many of which have been worked for generations by the same families. Neighbors get together for church suppers, family reunions, and summer picnics. There is a warmth and friendliness among the people of the Heartland that is the same now as it was in "the good old days." It is as American as can be. I think of Dorothy with Toto, and her dear Aunt Emma and Uncle Henry.

The Native Americans who first lived in the Heartland were familiar with its abundance. The forests and plains were full of game, and the lakes were home to many kinds of fish. Later, settlers came to the Heartland to farm, many of them from the tamed eastern parts of America. Others came from Europe, as Germans and Scandinavians found a climate much like that of their homes. Grain grew well in this region. Cattle thrived here, and soon the dairies were making cheeses to rival those of Europe. Although in many places the winters were cold and the growing season short, the soil was rich and farms prospered. Almost every little village, no matter how small, has its grain elevator standing tall against the deep blue of the sky. The hardworking people of this region have a tradition of substantial, tasty food, and the beer made from their golden grain is famed throughout the world.

Thanksgiving Roast Turkey with Mushroom Sage Dressing

Thanksgiving is a national holiday that unites all Americans in a most special way. It is a day when family and friends sit together and reflect on the many things we as Americans can be thankful for. The center of this celebration is traditionally a turkey feast. Benjamin Franklin had wanted the turkey to be our national emblem instead of the eagle. Certainly, turkey is dearer to our stomachs! In our nation's heartland, with its endless, beautiful, rich farm lands, Thanksgiving dinner is the height of American tradition. Mushrooms have long been hunted in Heartland forests and are popular in Thanksgiving turkey dressings.

Roast Turkey

1	fresh turkey (12–15 pounds)
	salt, pepper, and paprika
¼	cup butter, melted

Mushroom Sage Dressing

½	cup butter
¾	cup chopped onion (1 large)
1	medium loaf good-quality day-old white bread, torn into small pieces (to make about 8–9 cups)
1½	cups chopped celery with leaves
3	tablespoons fresh minced parsley
2	tablespoons fresh or dried sage
	salt and pepper to taste
1	pound fresh sliced mushrooms (brown if available)

Turkey Gravy

¾ cup chopped onion (1 large)
1 cup chopped celery
3 tablespoons flour
1 bay leaf
salt and pepper to taste

To prepare the dressing, melt the ½ cup butter in a large (preferably iron) frying pan. Add ¾ cup onion and cook, stirring, just until limp. Add bread crumbs, celery, parsley, sage, salt, and pepper. Cook and stir-fry for about 10 minutes; the bread should be lightly browned. Remove from pan, place in a bowl, and refrigerate. To leave more time for fun on Thanksgiving, it is best to make the dressing the evening before (but do NOT put it into the turkey at this time!). If you like a moister dressing, just before stuffing the turkey add 1 cup stock or white wine and gently mix with bread mixture.

To prepare stock for gravy and dressing, place the neck and giblets (heart, liver, and gizzard) in a pan with 6 cups water, one chopped onion, 1 cup chopped celery, salt and pepper, and a bay leaf. Cover and simmer for one hour, then set aside.

To roast the turkey, pat the cavity dry using paper towels. Sprinkle with salt and pepper. Spoon the dressing loosely in the cavity and stitch or skewer to close turkey skin. Dressing expands while cooking, so if you have any left over, simply bake it in a well-oiled pan for 30 minutes at 350°. Place the turkey on a flat rack in a large flat roasting pan, breast side up. Sprinkle skin with salt, pepper, and paprika. Bake turkey 15–20 minutes for each pound. Baste turkey with melted butter about every 30 minutes. When cooked, the internal temperature on a meat thermometer (inserted into the meatiest part of the breast) should be 180°F. Do not overcook. Let the turkey rest on a warmed platter while you make the gravy.

To make gravy, remove the giblets from your "stock." Pour off fat from turkey pan, leaving 3 tablespoons. Slowly add 3 tablespoons flour and blend until smooth over medium heat. Slowly add while stirring 3 cups of your stock with salt and pepper to taste, stirring until smooth. This will take about 6 minutes. Chop the giblets and add to the gravy.

To serve: Garnish turkey platter with watercress or parsley. Remove stuffing from turkey and place in a warmed bowl. Slice turkey and serve with traditional Thanksgiving foods, such as mashed potatoes, yams, creamed onions, cranberry sauce, pumpkin pie, or whatever dishes are traditional in your family. For some, the best part of Thanksgiving is turkey sandwiches the next day.

Cathy's Mom's Great Pork and Sauerkraut

My friend Cathy Zadel, whose childhood was spent in the small Minnesota town of Sauk Centre, is a most ardent cook. She loves to tell me tales of her mother, who was also a gifted cook and loved to try new recipes. This was a favorite dinner at their home on cold, snowy winter nights.

	pork loin roast (3–4 pounds)
2	pounds sauerkraut (refrigerated, bottled, or canned)
1	large onion, chopped
6	red potatoes, whole if small or quartered if large
6	garlic cloves, peeled
2	tablespoons juniper berries
2	tablespoons caraway seed
	salt and pepper to taste
1	cup dry white wine
2	cups chicken broth

Rinse the sauerkraut well and drain. Put in a 10″ x 14″ roasting pan. Add everything except the roast. Mix together. Place roast in center of pan. Roast at 325° for 3 hours. Stir sauerkraut around several times and baste pork with pan juices. This will serve 4–6.

Milwaukee Beer Beef Party Stew

Milwaukee is a city that really enjoys beer and sports. It is home to many of America's most famous breweries, so it is only natural that its citizens enjoy using beer in their cooking. This stew can easily be made a day ahead for a party, and will be all the better as the flavors will have a chance to mellow.

3	pounds chuck, round, or stewing beef cut in 1½-inch cubes
¾	cup flour for dredging
4	tablespoons oil
5	large onions (any variety), peeled and sliced
3	cups beer
1	10½-ounce can beef bouillon
3	garlic cloves, peeled and minced
1	tablespoon minced parsley
	pinch of thyme
1	bay leaf
	salt and pepper to taste
1	tablespoon brown sugar
1	tablespoon wine vinegar

Pat the meat dry with paper towels and dredge in flour. Heat the oil in a heavy stew pot and brown the beef in batches. Bacon fat may be used instead of oil. When finished, set the beef aside, put the onions in the pot, and lightly brown, adding more oil if needed. Return beef to the pot. Add beer, bouillon, garlic, herbs, salt, and pepper. Stir well. Cover pot and bake in a 325° oven for 2½ hours or until meat is tender. During the last ten minutes of cooking, stir in the sugar and vinegar. It may be necessary to add additional beer during cooking if the liquid is not covering the beef. Serve the stew to 6 with boiled potatoes and mugs of cold beer.

Granny's Ham and Potato Gratin for a Crowd*

I am an unabashed Julia Child fan. I have all of her cookbooks, and their pages are very worn from my constant use. I have met Julia several times at various fund-raising cooking events. The first was in 1978 for Planned Parenthood on a rainy day in La Jolla. In spite of the inclement

---

* From *The Way to Cook* by Julia Child. Copyright © 1989 by Julia Child. Reprinted by permission of Alfred A. Knopf, Inc.

weather, there was standing room only. This American doyenne is generous with her time, and has been responsible for communicating to this country that cooking is a fun adventure! She always answers my letters and is helpful in every way. This recipe of Julia's, from *The Way to Cook*, is exemplary of flavorful American main dishes for company, pot-lucks, church suppers, or parties. I think this comfortable food belongs with the Heartland, as this miraculous woman is close to our nation's hearts.

Granny's Ham and Potato Gratin for a Crowd is a great crowd pleaser, as well as a deliciously economical one that needs only a copious salad, a loaf of bread, and a jug of light red wine to make the meal. This will make 18–24 servings.

10	pounds "boiling" potatoes
	salt
1½ to 2	quarts cooked ham, diced, thinly sliced, or ground to make 6–8 cups
4	cups coarsely grated cheese (Swiss or a mixture such as Swiss, mozzarella, Jack, and/or cheddar)

Garlic and Mustard Sauce

5	ounces (1¼ sticks) butter
1	cup all-purpose flour
6½	cups hot milk
	salt and freshly ground pepper
	a pinch of nutmeg
2	large cloves garlic, pureed
¼	cup Dijon-style prepared mustard
½	teaspoon thyme or sage

Special Equipment Suggested

A food processor (useful for slicing and grating); an 8-quart covered kettle; a heavy-bottomed 3-quart saucepan for the sauce; a buttered 6-quart baking dish about 3 inches deep for the final dish.

The Potatoes

Have ready the kettle containing 4 cups salted cold water to cover. Peel the potatoes and slice them ¼ inch thick, dropping them into the cold water as you do so. Cover the kettle, and bring to the boil. Uncover and boil slowly 3–4 minutes until barely cooked through—eat several slices to check. Drain, cover the kettle again for 3–4 minutes to firm up the potato slices, then uncover.

The Garlic and Mustard Sauce (about 8 cups)

Cook the butter and flour together in a 3-quart saucepan over moderate heat until they foam and froth for 2 minutes without coloring. Remove from heat. Pour in half of the hot milk, whisking vigorously to blend thoroughly as you pour in the rest. Simmer 3 minutes, stirring. Remove from heat and whisk in the seasonings; bring to a simmer again, taste carefully, and add additional seasonings to taste.

To Assemble

Spoon a 1/16-inch layer of sauce on the bottom of the buttered baking dish. Set aside 3 cups of sauce and 1 cup of cheese for the topping. Now, to arrange everything in 4 layers, start with a quarter of the potatoes, then a quarter of the ham, followed by a third of the sauce, and sprinkle on a third of the cheese. Continue in layers, finishing the final layer with the remaining potatoes and ham. Spread on the reserved 3 cups of sauce to cover completely, then the last cup of cheese.

This may be prepared a day in advance—cover when cool and refrigerate. The final baking will be about 45 minutes at 375°. An hour or so before you plan to serve, preheat the oven to 375°. Bake in the upper third level just until the potatoes are bubbling hot and the top has browned nicely. This may be kept warm uncovered on a hot tray, but be sure not to overheat or the potatoes and ham will dry out.

Swiss Steak

My mother made Swiss steak and my mother-in-law made it too. Swiss steak is in almost every American cookbook and is certainly a Midwest favorite. It is easy and hearty. I like mine with mashed potatoes, but some prefer noodles. This is one of those dishes that is improved by preparing a day ahead.

2	pounds round steak, about ½ inch thick
½	cup flour, mixed with salt and pepper to taste
3	tablespoons vegetable or canola oil
3	tablespoons butter
1	large onion, sliced thinly (about 1 cup)
2	cloves garlic, minced
2	cups water
1	14-ounce can diced or whole tomatoes
2	carrots, cut in half
½	cup red or white wine (optional)
	minced parsley for garnish

Cut the steak into serving-size pieces. Mix the flour with salt and pepper in a flat pan. Dredge each piece of the steak, rubbing in the flour. Heat the oil and butter in a large frying pan. Fry each piece of steak until brown on each side, adding additional butter and oil as needed. Remove to a large baking casserole. When all the meat is browned, add the sliced onion and garlic to pan and stir-fry until limp. Add to the meat. Place 2 cups of water in the frying pan and stir to gather up juices left in pan. Add to meat along with tomatoes, carrots, and wine if used. Add additional water or stock if liquid does not cover the meat. Cover and bake at 350° for 1½ hours or until meat is tender. This may also be done on top of the stove, but I think the oven gives a better flavor. To serve, garnish with parsley and serve with mashed potatoes (or noodles) to 4.

Swedish Meatballs

The Swedish immigrants who came to the northern part of this country's heartland brought many delicious recipes from their homeland. Many of these recipes, like Swedish meatballs, quickly became a part of the American cuisine. These flavorful morsels still fill many a buffet table in all the states. The key to making excellent meatballs is to select quality meats. Pick out lean cuts of veal, pork, and beef, and ask your butcher to grind them for you.

½	pound lean pork
½	pound veal
½	pound lean beef
2	tablespoons butter
1	medium onion, finely diced (¾ cup)
1	egg
½	cup milk
1	cup white bread, broken in small pieces (2–3 slices)
	salt and pepper to taste
½	teaspoon nutmeg

For frying: 2 tablespoons butter plus 1 tablespoon vegetable oil
For gravy: 2 tablespoons flour, 2 cups half-and-half

Melt the 2 tablespoons butter in a 10- to 12-inch frying pan. Fry the onion just until limp, and set aside. Mix egg and milk and add bread. Let sit 10 minutes for bread to absorb the liquids. In a large bowl combine the meat, seasonings, and onion. Then combine this with the egg mixture. (I use my hands for this, to make sure the mixture is smooth and completely mixed.) This may be done ahead and refrigerated.

In a 10- to 12-inch frying pan (you may use original pan, just make sure there are not any onion bits remaining), heat the butter and oil until hot but not smoking. Using your hands, roll the meat mixture into balls about the size of a walnut. Fry, turning and shaking the pan, for about 15 minutes. The meatballs should be brown on all sides. Remove from pan. Make a gravy by adding 2 tablespoons flour to the pan. Stir flour around to gather up any meat drippings. Slowly add 2 cups half-and-half with salt and pepper to taste. Serve on top of meatballs.

This will make about 24 meatballs. For dinner, it will serve 4. Serve with mashed potatoes. For appetizers, place on a platter and serve with toothpicks.

Delilah's Utah Casserole

My mother-in-law Maureen was born in the small town of Payson in northern Utah. She had come to Long Beach as a bride, but always returned to her home town for a part of every year to visit with the large family. In later years, Maureen was able to move back permanently to this place she loved. When at 84 she passed away, there was a large church service and graveyard burial. At the end of the ceremonies, all the family and many friends returned to her home. We arrived to find gifts of ready-to-eat food from family and friends filling the table. Everyone was able to share in the feast and the memories of a special lady. One of my favorites was this tasty casserole from her friend Delilah.

- 2 cups uncooked potatoes, cut in strips (about 2½″ x ½″)
- 1 cup carrots, cut in strips
- 1 6½-ounce can chopped clams
- 1 medium onion, peeled and sliced
- 1 stick butter (4 ounces)
- salt and pepper to taste
- ½ teaspoon dill seed or weed

Lightly grease a 2-quart baking casserole. Place the potato strips in the bottom. Next add the carrots, followed by clams with juice, and finally the onion. Melt the butter with seasonings and pour over casserole. Bake at 350°, covered, for 45 minutes. Remove cover. Sprinkle with paprika and fresh parsley, if desired. This will serve 4.

German Apple Pancakes

Big hearty breakfasts are truly appreciated in the Heartland, especially during the long cold winters. Served with strong hot coffee, this Minnesota recipe wins raves every time. It is especially good when accompanied by smoked or pork sausage!

- 4 eggs
- ¾ cup flour
- ¾ cup milk
- ½ teaspoon salt
- 4 tablespoons butter
- 2 cooking apples (Granny Smith or green), thinly sliced
- ¼ cup sugar
- ¼ teaspoon cinnamon

Heat oven to 400°. Place two 8-inch round layer cake pans in the oven for 5 minutes. Beat eggs, flour, milk, and salt in mixer bowl (or in food processor) at medium speed for 1 minute. Remove heated pans from oven. Place 2 tablespoons butter in each one and rotate pans until butter melts and coats sides of pans. Arrange half of apple slices in each pan. Mix sugar and cinnamon and divide between the pans, sprinkling over apples. Pour batter in pans so each has the same amount. Bake uncovered for 20–25 minutes or until puffed and golden. Cut in wedges. Serve hot, topped with syrup, applesauce, cream, powdered sugar, or fruit. This will serve 4.

Minnesota Wild Rice with Mushrooms

The wild, beautiful Minnesota lakes are the home of the celebrated gourmet wild rice. Native Ojibway Indians harvest much of this rice, and it is an important part of their diet. The special flavor and texture of wild rice make this dish popular throughout the Heartland.

2	cups cooked and drained wild rice
¼	cup butter
½	pound brown or white fresh mushrooms, sliced
3	green onions, finely minced
	salt and pepper to taste
	parsley for garnish

Cook the rice according to package directions, drain well, and set aside. This may be done ahead and refrigerated. In a frying pan, melt the butter over a low flame. Add the mushrooms and onions, and fry just until limp. Add rice, salt, and pepper. Stir, blending ingredients together, until rice is hot. Garnish with parsley. This will serve 4.

Chicago Polish Asparagus

Chicago, famed as "the windy city," has the largest Polish population of any city in the world including cities in Poland. Polish cooking is hearty and flavorful. Poland and Chicago both have severe winters, and the coming of spring is a joyous event. Asparagus is a part of the Polish springtime celebration. This recipe is easy and brings out the best of the fresh, pert flavor of asparagus.

- 3 pounds fresh thin to medium asparagus stalks
- ¼ cup butter (½ stick)
- 5 tablespoons white bread crumbs
- salt and pepper to taste
- pinch of sugar

Wash asparagus and discard tough bottom stem. This is easily done by holding the stalk and snapping the top from the bottom; it will break naturally at the right place. Fill a large pot with water and bring to a boil. Add asparagus and boil, uncovered, over a medium flame for about 10 minutes. While asparagus is cooking, melt the butter in a pan, add crumbs and seasonings, and lightly brown. Drain the asparagus immediately and lay on a warm serving platter. Spoon the crumbs over the top. This will serve 6.

Golden Glow Salad

While it is true that Jello™ may not be as popular as it was in the days when refrigerators were a novelty, this cherished American salad is still refreshing, and its shimmering golden glow is to be found on Heartland tables to this day.

- 1 3-ounce package lemon Jello™
- 1½ cups boiling water
- 1 8-ounce can crushed pineapple
- 1½ cups fresh grated carrots
- ½ cup mayonnaise
- ¼ cup toasted chopped pecans

Place the Jello™ powder in a bowl. Pour in the hot water and stir to dissolve. Add entire contents (with juice) of pineapple can. Stir in carrots. Let cool slightly. Pour into a 1½-quart mold and place in refrigerator to set (several hours or overnight). Stir once or twice while setting to evenly distribute carrots and pineapple. Unmold and place on a bed of lettuce. Dribble mayonnaise over salad and sprinkle pecans on top. This will serve 6.

Kansas Potato Salad

This simple potato salad recipe was handed down to our good friend Dr. Harold Clark by his mother. Her presentation of this family recipe (shared here in its original form) is charming and reflects America as it was before World War II:

"I use new potatoes if possible, and cook them in the jackets. For two people, and when I do not want any left over, I cook only three small ones. They will cook in 25 to 28 minutes. I let them cool a bit and then peel off the jackets and dice them. Then while they are still quite warm I add 1 T. vinegar and some salt and pepper. By the time they are cold the vinegar will be absorbed. Of course, as you increase the amount of potatoes, increase the vinegar.

"I use two hard-boiled eggs for the above amount. These are added when the potatoes are cold. Sometimes I mix my salad an hour or so before dinner. If you wish to mix ahead of time and put in the refrigerator, be sure to cover. Personally I do not like potato salad too cold, that is why I do not put it in the refrigerator for more than an hour or maybe not at all.

"I use Miracle Whip. I use a tiny, and I do mean tiny, bit of green pepper cut in very small pieces, and I like to add some slivers of pimento for color. I also add 1 onion about the size of a good-sized egg. I like the flavor the white onions give. They are better in potato salad than young green onions or Spanish onions or yellow onions, to my way of thinking, altho sometimes if I think I don't have enough onion in the salad, I do add some green onion and maybe a little bit on the top, but very little. Use enough Miracle Whip to moisten, and probably add more pepper and salt. I do a bit of tasting here. I think as much as anything one needs to get enough, and just enough, onion in potato salad. Harold's grandmother made extra good potato salad and I decided she was using more onion than I had been using. Mine was better ever after. Of course, the hard-boiled eggs are added before the Miracle Whip. One can vary this by adding celery or cuke, but I seldom do. We seem to like the plain kind."

Farm Buttermilk Biscuits

Early Heartland farm wives used sour milk as a leavening agent, but it did not always work well. When commercial baking powder was introduced in the 1860s, it immediately became popular for home baking. Biscuits are a favorite in all our states but have always been a staple on farm tables.

- 2 cups flour
- 2 teaspoons baking powder
- ¼ teaspoon baking soda
- 1 teaspoon salt
- ¼ cup vegetable shortening
- ¾ cup buttermilk

It is important that biscuits go in a very hot oven, so preheat your oven to 450°. Sift dry ingredients together. Cut in shortening until mixture is crumbly. A chef once told me the mixture should be like oatmeal flakes. Gradually add buttermilk, mixing just until batter is smooth. Knead dough lightly and quickly on a floured surface. Roll or pat out dough to a thickness of about ½ inch for thick biscuits or ¼ inch for thinner, crustier biscuits. Cut into circles with a biscuit cutter. Place close together on an ungreased baking sheet. Bake for 10–12 minutes until golden brown. Serve immediately. This will make about 15 to 20 (depending on size) biscuits. A nice variation is chive biscuits; simply add 4 tablespoons to dry ingredients after sifting.

"The Toasts": Cinnamon, French, and Get-Well Milk

The Heartland is the wheat basket of our nation. The first time I crossed the country, it was late spring. We drove through endless fields of grain in a flat landscape. The skyline was pierced here and there with tall grain silos. In Kansas, there were most pleasant roadside rest areas, each with picnic tables and a sign adorned with a sunflower (the state flower) to denote that this was a Kansas undertaking for their visitors.

Americans need the grain from the Heartland for their enormous bread consumption. Sandwiches are number one on our lunch menu. There is bread with breakfast and dinner, and then we have the "toasts."

Cinnamon Toast

Cinnamon toast is a favorite with hot chocolate on a nippy evening. For 2 servings you will need:

- 4 slices good-quality white bread (good quality is from a bakery or is a superior supermarket brand)
- 3 tablespoons butter, at room temperature
- ⅓ cup sugar
- 1 teaspoon cinnamon

Mix the sugar and cinnamon together. Toast bread on one side. Remove and butter untoasted side. Sprinkle with the cinnamon/sugar mixture. Place under broiler just until the top is bubbly. A popular accompaniment is a small portion of applesauce.

French Toast

French toast is popular with most young people. Once, for my youngest daughter's birthday slumber party, I made this for breakfast. There were 10 young ladies who devoured the toast quicker than I could cook it.

- 2 eggs
- dash of salt
- ⅔ cup milk
- 6 slices day-old bread (it holds together better than fresh)
- butter for frying, about ¼ cup

Beat eggs together with the milk and salt in a shallow bowl. Dip pieces of bread in this mixture. Melt the butter in a frying pan over a medium flame. Fry bread on both sides. Butter gives the flavor. This will serve 2. Top with butter, cinnamon, syrup, jelly, or jam.

Get-Well Milk Toast

When I was a young girl and recovering from some sort of childhood malady, my Nana would say to my mother, "Give that child some milk toast." I was always eager for this comforting nourishment.

M.F.K. Fisher writes about milk toast in *An Alphabet for Gourmets* and mentions a lack of recipes for it in cookbooks. Of course, you do not need to be a cooking wizard to prepare milk toast; however, it is an important American comfort recipe, and I wanted it in this book.

- 2 cups milk
- 2 teaspoons butter, at room temperature
- pinch of salt and pepper
- 4 slices good-quality bread

Place milk, butter, and salt in a saucepan. Heat over a low flame just until butter melts. It is important not to overcook the milk, as you do not want a disagreeable burnt-milk flavor. Toast the bread on both sides. Take two warmed, shallow bowls. Place two slices of bread in each bowl. Cover with the milk and serve immediately to 2, with spoons.

Indiana Devil's Food Coffee Cake

I collect cookbooks, and am especially interested in our nation's culinary trends. One cake that has never lost popularity is devil's food. This curious name seems to have something to do with a rather puritanical American thought that devouring rich chocolate food is bad. Angel food cakes are pure white and do not contain anything but light, delicate ingredients, so they are deemed sort of heavenly. Both are long-standing favorites in the American cake menu.

I have friends whose relatives in Indiana regularly attend family reunion picnics. This recipe, from one of those Indiana cousins, is always a favorite at these happy gatherings. The coffee adds to the flavor and texture of the cake.

2	cups flour
1	teaspoon baking powder
1	teaspoon soda
1	teaspoon salt
1	teaspoon cinnamon
½	cup cocoa
1½	cups sugar
½	cup vegetable shortening
⅔	cup buttermilk
½	cup cooled strong coffee
2	eggs
1	teaspoon vanilla

Sift dry ingredients together in a mixing bowl. Add shortening, ⅓ cup buttermilk, and coffee all at once. Beat for 2 minutes until batter is smooth. Next add remaining ⅓ cup buttermilk, 2 eggs, and vanilla. Beat for 2 minutes. Pour into two lightly greased and floured 8-inch layer cake pans and bake at 350° for 30–35 minutes. Cake should bounce back when pressed with finger. Remove from pan and cool on racks. Frost with your favorite cake frosting, or enjoy it plain.

Illinois Lincoln Thanksgiving Pumpkin Pie

Our family once drove from New York to Los Angeles in a secondhand Volkswagen bus. We camped out each night, all the way across the country. We were returning with our three children, all under the age of 10, after two years of living in Rome. It was fun to be home again, and I was impressed with the nostalgic moods of the American camping sites. One of our overnight stops was in the New Salem State Park in Illinois. There, we visited the small cabin where Abraham Lincoln and his family lived during his early adult years. It was here that the future president began studying law. This small town, on a wooded grove above the Sangamon River, has been restored for the nation to view. The visit left me feeling a bit closer to this great visionary president.

During the tragic times of the Civil War, President Lincoln heeded the letters of Mrs. Sarah Hale, who for twenty years had begged the government to declare Thanksgiving a legally "hallowed and exalted" day. Americans had always celebrated Thanksgiving, but it was not a national holiday until 1863 when President Lincoln proclaimed the last Thursday in November as a day of thanksgiving.

When we lived in Paris, I thought it would be fun to have a Thanksgiving dinner for our American student friends. In the street market on Rue Lepic, I purchased what I thought was a pumpkin and made a pie. Everyone was most impressed until they took a bite and found it tasted like soap. It was obvious that what I had bought was not a pumpkin, but some bizarre kind of French squash. This recipe, though, is the classic pumpkin pie.

1	9-inch unbaked pastry crust of your choice*
1½	cups canned or fresh cooked, strained pumpkin
¾	cup half-and-half
2	eggs, beaten
⅔	cup brown sugar
½	teaspoon each ground ginger, ground nutmeg, and salt
¼	teaspoon ground cloves
	fresh whipped cream for topping

Combine ingredients in a bowl. Blend well and pour into the piecrust. Bake at 400° for 55 minutes. Spoon whipped cream on top. This will serve 6.

Wichita Peanut Butter and Jelly Cookies

Americans have a passion for the combination of peanut butter and jelly, from the children who clamor for it in sandwiches for school lunch, to adults who savor a kind of guilty childlike pleasure in the same sandwiches. George Carver pioneered the planting of peanuts in soil that was worn out from cotton planting, and a doctor in St. Louis in the early 1900s invented peanut butter as a high-protein, easily digested food for his patients.

*For basic piecrust recipe, see "Washington Apple Pie" in The Northwest and Alaska section. For a single crust, use one-half ingredient amounts.

While driving across the country on a hot summer day, we stopped at a Wichita cafe. It was blessedly cool inside, and the friendly waitress suggested we taste some of their homemade cookies. With a chilled glass of milk, they made a refreshing interlude in our long drive. When we finally got home to California, I made my own version of this Kansas cookie.

- ½ cup shortening (can be part butter)
- ½ cup peanut butter, smooth or crunchy
- 1 cup sugar
- 1 egg
- 2 tablespoons milk
- 1 teaspoon vanilla
- ½ teaspoon baking powder
- 1¾ cups all-purpose flour
- ½ cup jam, your favorite flavor

Cream shortening, peanut butter, and sugar together. Add egg, milk, and vanilla and blend well. Sift baking powder and flour together, add to dough, and mix well. Chill in a bowl (for easier handling) for about 15 minutes.

Roll dough into 1-inch balls. Place on an ungreased cookie sheet about 2 inches apart. With your finger, press an indentation in the center of each cookie, and place a small dab of jam in the dent. Do not overfill, or the jam will run out and burn on the cookie sheet. Bake at 375° for 12–15 minutes, until golden brown. Remove and cool on a rack. This will make about 3½ dozen tasty cookies.

All-American Brownies

The brownie is an all-American favorite. This recipe is the basic quick and easy version, a good recipe for young children to make as a fun early cooking lesson. There are many recipes for gooey rich brownies with glossy frostings, but really, is there anything better than just a simple brownie with a glass of milk?

2	squares unsweetened chocolate (1 ounce each)
⅓	cup butter or shortening or mixture of both
2	eggs
1	cup sugar (white or brown)
1	teaspoon vanilla
¾	cup flour
1	teaspoon baking powder
½	teaspoon salt
¾	cup chopped walnuts

Melt butter or shortening and chocolate in a heavy pan over very low heat. Set aside. In a bowl, beat the eggs until light, then add sugar gradually. Next add chocolate mixture and vanilla—this may be done with a mixer or by hand. Sift flour, baking powder, and salt, mix into egg-chocolate mixture, and blend in walnuts. Place in a buttered 8″ x 8″ or 9″ x 9″ square pan. Bake at 350° for 30–35 minutes. Do not overbake or brownies will be dry. Remove from oven and cool on a rack. While slightly warm, cut into desired size squares.

Heartland Drinks

Our Heartland is the domain of all-American liquid refreshments. My friend Kriss Erickson, a former Heartland resident, has offered recipes for favorites from this extraordinary region. Kriss was a bartender in the Heartland, and is a master in this field!

One of Kriss' hints is that it is important to use the right size glass for preparing drinks. His recommendations for use in your home bar are: old-fashioned glasses (10-ounce), highball glasses (12-ounce), and collins glasses (14-ounce).

Bourbon Highball

Fill an old-fashioned glass with ice. Add:

1½	ounces bourbon
	ginger ale to fill glass

Bourbon Press

Fill a highball glass with ice. Add:

- 1 ounce (shot) bourbon
- splash of 7-Up
- club soda to fill glass

Whiskey Sour

Fill an old-fashioned glass with ice. Add:

- 1 ounce (shot) whiskey
- half sweet-and-sour and half 7-Up to fill glass
- lime slice for garnish

Tom Collins

Fill a collins glass with ice. Add:

- 2 ounces gin
- 2 ounces sweet-and-sour
- 2 ounces club soda
- maraschino cherry and orange slice for garnish

Gin Rickey

Fill a highball glass with ice. Add:

- 1 ounce (shot) gin
- splash of 7-Up
- splash of lime juice
- club soda to fill glass
- lime slice for garnish

The Northwest and Alaska

Alaska and the great Northwest are a continuance of our nation's pioneer spirit. Americans are still migrating to these areas in search of fresh air, silent places, endless seacoast, meandering orchards, grand landscapes, towering snow-capped mountains, and cool green forests. These migrants' fortitude and zeal for life are evident in the Northwest. In Alaska, we met couples who had come to begin a new life, and single individuals who were finding a niche, a sort of last frontier.

In Washington's Seattle Pike Place Market, much of the bounty of the Northwest and Alaska is on display and for sale. I was amazed that there could be so many varieties of salmon. The hues range from nearly white to a deep red. They are arranged with care on crunchy ice in a beautiful rosy spectrum. The informative fish vendors told me the remarkable qualities of each variety. These colorful market characters took great delight in explaining the virtues of clams, crabs, oysters, shrimp, halibut, and other shimmering fish from these deep waters. The fruit and vegetable counters had vibrant displays of berries, mushrooms, apples, cherries, pears, hazelnuts, honey, and locally homemade jams and jellies. A pear saleslady told me that one-fourth of all the pears eaten in America come from the Northwest.

My experience in Alaska on a salmon fishing trip left me with memories of giant mountains, rocky seacoasts, and wide rivers. I caught a glimpse of a moose in the woods and bald eagles resting on a huge tree. From our friend's little fishing boat on the Kenai Peninsula, I could see the salmon cruising about in the cold green-blue waters below. Near Homer, I tasted a very delicious pristine halibut for lunch. It had been caught that morning. The flesh looked like a shiny white pearl. It did not need sauces or seasonings—the flavor was the very essence of the sea. The giant crabs for sale in the Alaskan fish market looked like some science fiction movie fantasy. For our nation's many seafood lovers, the Northwest is certainly the place to be.

Anchorage Broiled Halibut with Olive-Cheese Topping

Halibut fresh from Alaska is the very best. When we visited friends in Anchorage, the four of us took their comfy motor home for several days of fishing on the Kenai Peninsula. On the way, we stopped near Homer for lunch, and I chose the broiled halibut. It may be difficult to imagine halibut flesh as a piece of art, but this was absolutely beautiful: shimmering, glistening, and translucently white, with a delicate sea-fresh flavor. I have never forgotten it.

In California, we can often purchase fresh Alaskan halibut. I like to prepare it with a little olive topping. I sent the recipe to my Alaskan friends, who loved it and said that in the dead of the Alaskan winter the olives remind them of sunny orchards.

1	1-pound halibut fillet (other fish may also be used)
4	tablespoons melted butter or olive oil
	juice of 1 lemon (about 2 tablespoons)
	salt and pepper to taste
3	tablespoons chopped black olives (canned is fine)
¼	cup grated Jack cheese

Mix the olives and grated cheese together and set aside. Combine the butter or olive oil with the lemon juice, add salt and pepper, and brush both sides of the halibut with this combination. Reserve any remaining liquid. Broil the halibut 3–4 inches from the heat, on both sides, until done (about 4–5 minutes per side, depending on the thickness of the fillet). The flesh should be white and flake easily. I like to place the halibut on a piece of foil, turning up the edges to keep all the juices in place. Remove from broiler and spoon the olive and cheese mixture, along with the reserved liquid, over the halibut. Return to the broiler and broil just until the cheese is melted, about a minute. This will serve 2, and is heavenly when accompanied by steamed red potatoes and fresh spinach.

Alaska State Fair Barbecued Spareribs

The annual Alaska State Fair is held in the fertile Matanuska Valley, where cabbages can grow up to 70 pounds in the short summer season. The rugged Chugach Mountain range that rises above the valley gives the whole fair a travel-poster look. As at any state fair, quilts, rabbits, and big zucchini are on display, but do-it-yourself log cabins and fur shoes add a distinctively local touch.

The food is hearty, and barbecued ribs, served fresh off the fire out of a big metal tub, are a popular favorite. Corn on the cob, a big serving of beans, and two paper napkins are the embellishments. Carefully, you carry your plate over to the "Sluice Box," a Quonset hut with long tables, beer, and a neighborhood Western band. Everyone there is chomping on ribs and having fun.

3–4	pounds beef or pork spareribs
2	tablespoons butter
1	onion, finely chopped
2	cloves garlic, minced
¾	cup ketchup
½	cup water
1	teaspoon mustard
	salt and pepper to taste

To make the barbecue sauce, melt the butter in a saucepan, add onion and garlic, and cook just until limp. Add remaining ingredients. Stir and simmer, uncovered, for 10 minutes. Barbecue the ribs on a grill over charcoal, basting with sauce.

The ribs may also be baked in the oven: Place ribs on a rack and cook for 30 minutes at 425°. Pour off fat carefully. Turn down oven to 375° and cook ribs an additional 30 minutes, basting several times with sauce. This will serve 4.

Steaks with Oregon Blue Cheese Topping

Blue cheese salad dressings are popular nationwide, and that is the way most Americans are familiar with this cheese. The state of Oregon is a famous blue cheese producer. One of my friends moved from California to Oregon, and raves about the quiet and beauty there. This recipe is one she sent to me using her adopted state's famous dairy product. The lively flavors are perfect with steak.

- 4 steaks (¾ to 1 pound each—rib eye, New York, or top sirloin)
- ¼ cup blue cheese, at room temperature
- ¼ cup sweet butter, at room temperature
- 1 clove garlic, minced
- salt and freshly ground pepper to taste

Combine cheese, butter, and garlic. Mash into a paste with a fork. Sprinkle the steaks with salt and pepper to taste. Preheat your broiler. Broil the steak about 2 inches from the heat. The amount of time will depend on the thickness, usually about 6 minutes on each side. Pull out the broiler pan, turn steaks, and spread the tasty topping over the surfaces. Return to broiler and finish cooking until desired doneness. This will serve 4.

Blue Cheese Appetizer Dip

Use the same recipe for the cheese, butter, and garlic as above, but add ¼ cup sour cream. This makes a very nice appetizer spread or dip. It may also be used to fill the center of celery ribs for a refreshing nibble.

The All-American Hamburger

Hamburgers are consumed everywhere in our country. It seems to be the food associated with international impressions of what America eats, and sometimes Americans are looked down upon gastronomically for this casual food. Hamburgers need defending! If one analyzes a hamburger, there is nothing but tasty ingredients all layered together. They are always appetizing and, in spite of health doomsayers, are balanced and nutritious. I thought of this when I was in Alaska, our most northern state. I was in a rustic cafe and most of the customers (Eskimos, tourists, and locals) were eating hamburgers with French fries. Bottles of catsup and mustard adorned the plastic tablecloths. Americans adore this national dish, and if anything unites the American people it is the hamburger.

Hamburgers originated in the German seaport city of Hamburg. German immigrants coming to America brought this recipe for a "Hamburg-style chopped steak." There is a dispute about who made the first hamburger in America. Louis Lassen is recorded as serving the first "burger" at his Connecticut luncheonette in 1890, but then there is Carlie Nagreen, whose relatives claim that he sold hamburgers from his ox-drawn food stand at the Outgamie County Fair in 1885. This debate will surely continue among hamburger scholars.

Of course, there are hamburgers and there are hamburgers—some well made and some not-so-well made. The key to a good hamburger is that the ingredients should be fresh and of good quality. Both my mother and my mother-in-law always had the butcher grind their hamburger beef fresh. It only takes a minute to politely ask your local butcher to grind either round or chuck steak for you. He or she will not mind—this is part of their job. With freshly ground beef you know exactly what is in your hamburger. This recipe is for four hamburgers but may easily be enlarged. Hamburgers are a casual affair, and some may like onions and not tomatoes, so there is always a choice of ingredients.

4	freshly baked hamburger buns
1	pound freshly ground chuck or round steak
	salt and pepper to taste
1	tablespoon butter or oil, if burgers are to be fried
	onion slices
	tomato slices
	cheddar cheese slices
	pickle slices or relish
	mayonnaise
	ketchup
	iceberg lettuce

To begin, assemble all the ingredients on a platter so you will have them on hand to construct your hamburgers. The buns should be heated or toasted. If desired, the cheese may be placed on the buns while they are heated if you like really melted cheese.

Mix the ground beef with salt and pepper. Form into 4 flattish patties that will fit your hamburger buns. I like to cook hamburgers in an iron frying pan. To do this, heat the pan for 3 minutes. Place the butter or oil in the pan. Fry patty on each side until brown and cooked to your taste. If broiling, simply place on foil under broiler and broil on each side. If using an outside barbecue grill, cook on each side, turning once.

Place cooked hamburger on the bottom section of bun. Add desired ingredients. Gently press top of bun on assembled ingredients. Eat while hot and enjoy this American classic.

Alaskan Sourdough Starter

Alaskan gold prospectors were nicknamed "sourdoughs" because a container of starter was part of their mining gear. To understand the importance of sourdough starter, one must remember that gold miners, settlers, explorers, and pioneer families did not have a bakery around the corner. Baked goods had to be prepared in the untamed wilderness. A sourdough starter is simply a mixture of milk or water with flour that captures airborne yeast and acts as a leavening agent for baking. On cold

Alaskan winter nights, the starter would be taken to bed so it would stay warm for making pancakes the following morning. Another use for sourdough starter unrelated to pancakes is for tanning hides. The starter is rubbed into the inside of small hides such as mink, ermine, or muskrat.

To Make Your Own Starter

- 2 cups flour
- 3 tablespoons sugar
- 1 teaspoon salt
- 1 package dry yeast
- 2 cups lukewarm water

Mix dry ingredients together in a mixing bowl (not metal). Add lukewarm water and stir. Cover with cheesecloth and place in a warm place (80°–85°). Stir starter a few times a day. In two days, the mixture should have bubbles and a nice sour smell. This is due to carbon dioxide gas that will raise and flavor your dough. It will be ready to use. Store in glass or crockery. Remember, if you remove 1 cup of starter you must replace it with 1 cup of fresh ingredients (I use flour mixed with milk to a pancake batter consistency). The starter may be refrigerated. To use again, be sure to let it come to room temperature. You will notice that a yellowish liquid may form on top of your starter. Just stir it in—this is "hooch," a crude alcoholic liquid. Sometimes, desperate gold miners would drink this if they did not have any alcoholic beverages nearby. Commercial starters are sold in Alaska and may also be used. Follow package directions.

Sourdough Blueberry Pancakes

Blueberries (a favorite Alaskan berry) and the tang of sourdough are a perfect combination for a happy morning breakfast. Notice that this must be started the night before!

½	cup sourdough starter
2	cups flour
2	cups lukewarm water
2	tablespoons sugar
1	teaspoon salt
½	teaspoon baking powder
3	tablespoons melted butter or cooking oil
2	eggs, beaten
1	cup blueberries (fresh, frozen, or drained canned)
½	teaspoon baking soda mixed with 1 tablespoon water

Place the starter in a bowl. Next add flour and water. Stir until mixture is smooth. Place in a warm place in your kitchen overnight. To prepare the pancakes, add sugar, salt, baking powder, and butter or oil to batter. Blend in eggs and blueberries and lastly the soda. Mix lightly. Cook on a lightly greased pancake griddle over medium heat. This will make 4 generous servings. Serve with butter, syrup, or honey. Sausage or bacon make a pleasant accompaniment.

Seattle Art Museum's Salade Niçoise Northwest

Seattle does have rain; however, it is gentle, and a rainy day is a good time to visit Seattle's stunning art museum. It is one of the finest in our country, renowned for regional art and Northwest Coast Native American artifacts. Time passes quickly in this stimulating museum. When you are hungry, the museum has a most attractive cafe with outstanding food. The menu reflects all the flavors of this alluring region. I was delighted with a most appetizing northwestern version of Niçoise salad. The cafe chef, Steven Iverson, kindly offered to share the recipe. This type of salad may be used for a main course for lunch or dinner.

Dressing

1	2-ounce can anchovies
3	tablespoons Dijon-style mustard (grainy recommended)
7	fresh garlic cloves, peeled

Process in a food processor or blender until smooth.

Add:

    1¾   cups balsamic vinegar
    1   teaspoon sugar

Process until smooth.

Next Add:

    2½   cups good-quality olive oil
    5   cups canola or other vegetable oil
        salt to taste
        freshly ground pepper to taste (about 2 teaspoons)

Blend or process all ingredients until smooth. Remove to a container. I use a tall glass jar. This makes over 2 quarts of dressing. It may be used as needed and is delicious with everything. You will be pleased to have made this large amount.

Salad Ingredients (for 4 generous servings)

    2   pounds red potatoes
    4   tablespoons olive oil
    2   tablespoons fresh or dried rosemary leaves
    1   pound fresh string beans
    1   cup thinly sliced red pepper, battonnet cut
    1   cup thinly sliced yellow pepper, battonnet cut
    1   cup red onion, battonnet cut
    2   pounds fish fillets, cut in 4 serving pieces (halibut, salmon, or tuna)
    4   tablespoons capers for garnish

Wash potatoes and place in a shallow roasting pan. Drizzle olive oil over potatoes. Sprinkle the rosemary over all. Roast at 400° until tender, stirring now and then (about one hour). Set aside. Cook string beans in 1 quart salted boiling water for 8 minutes. Drain immediately and set aside. Cut peppers and onions in battonnets (strips approximately 2½ inches long and ½ inch wide).

This is a composed salad, which simply means you arrange the ingredients in an attractive manner. To do this, take 4 plates and divide the potatoes among them. I like to quarter them. The ingredients may be served chilled or at room temperature. Arrange remaining ingredients (except the fish) around potatoes.

The last step is to place the fish on a grill or under a broiler. Lightly brush with olive oil or melted butter. Cook on one side and then the other until golden brown. The time will vary with the fish. Sprinkle salt and pepper to taste over surface. Place the fillet across the salad. Pour the dressing (to individual taste) over each salad. Garnish with capers and serve at once. The delight of this salad is the warm fish mixed with the Provençal-flavored salad.

Baked Alaska

The United States purchased the Alaska Territory from Russia in 1867, inspiring this dramatic, classically American dessert. The recipe was invented at New York's famed Delmonico's restaurant in 1876; the meringue topping, with the help of a little imagination, is supposed to look like snow-covered Alaskan mountain peaks. When I was a young bride, this dessert was one of the first recipes that seemed a formidable challenge to prepare. The photo in my cookbook looked so spectacular I could hardly wait to try it. Of course, I was quite nervous and worried that the ice cream would melt all over my oven. To my amazement, it all came out perfectly the first time and our dinner guests were most impressed. The only things you have to remember are to preheat your oven and to have the meringue topping all prepared. You will need:

	Hot Milk Easy Cake
1	quart strawberry ice cream (or other)
	meringue

Hot Milk Easy Cake

- 1 teaspoon vanilla
- 2 eggs
- 1 cup sugar
- 1 cup flour
- 1 teaspoon baking powder
- ¼ teaspoon salt
- ½ cup milk
- 1 tablespoon butter

Beat the vanilla and eggs together until slightly thick. Slowly add sugar and mix. Sift together the flour, baking powder, and salt. Add to the first mixture, blending until smooth. Heat the milk and butter just until the butter melts. Add immediately to flour mixture (mix in quickly) and blend. (Don't worry, the batter is supposed to be thin.) Place in an 8- or 9-inch buttered and floured square cake pan, and bake at 350° for 25 minutes. A toothpick poked into the cake should come out clean. Remove cake from oven and turn out of pan onto a cooling rack until needed.

Ice Cream

I have found you need to reshape your ice cream. Let the ice cream sit out until you can easily remove it from the carton. Place into an 8-inch stainless steel bowl. Press down, cover with foil and place in the freezer until needed. This will fit on top of the cake.

Meringue

- 4 egg whites, at room temperature
- ⅛ teaspoon cream of tartar
- ½ cup sugar

Beat egg whites and cream of tartar together with an electric beater or wire whisk until foamy. Slowly sprinkle in sugar while beating until the mixture is stiff.

To Assemble

Place the cake on a piece of brown paper (a cut-up grocery bag is just fine) on a board. I use my breadboard. Place the ice cream on top of the cake. The idea is that you want the ice cream in a sort of neat mound on the cake. Cover with the meringue. (The breadboard should be large enough to allow about ½-inch margin around the meringue-covered cake.) Place in a preheated 500° oven for 3–5 minutes, just enough time for the meringue to brown. Immediately remove and bring to the table (on breadboard) and serve quickly before the ice cream melts and becomes a mess. Serve to 4. Baked Alaska is a memorably dramatic dessert.

Washington Apple Pie

Although apples are grown in nearly every state, Washington leads the nation in their cultivation, and the quality of Washington apples is exceptional. Apple pie is the ultimate American dessert, but it is also a good snack any time of the day. It may be topped with a scoop of vanilla ice cream or a wedge of sharp cheddar cheese. It can be especially fine to have a slice of this pie mid-morning with a cup of hot coffee.

Basic Crust for a Two-Crust Pie

- 2 cups flour
- 1 teaspoon salt
- ⅔ cup shortening or lard
- 3 tablespoons (more or less) cold liquid (ice water, milk, or orange juice)

Pie Filling

- 6–7 cups apples, peeled and cored, sliced lengthwise into ½-inch wedges
- 1 cup sugar
- 1½ teaspoons cornstarch or 2 tablespoons flour
- 1 teaspoon cinnamon
- ½ teaspoon nutmeg (optional)
- 1 tablespoon lemon juice
- 1–2 tablespoons butter

Place flour and salt in a bowl. Mix in shortening with a fork or pastry mixer until the mixture is broken up into small pea-sized pieces. Add liquid gradually. When mixture is slightly stiff, form into a ball with your hands. My mother-in-law Maureen, who taught me how to make a piecrust, always used cold milk as liquid for her excellent piecrusts. Flour a board, and divide dough into two balls. Roll one out for bottom crust. Dough should be rolled out to about ⅛ inch thick. Place in a 9-inch pie pan.

To prepare filling, mix the sugar, flour or cornstarch, cinnamon, and nutmeg (if used) in a bowl. Add the apple slices and lemon juice. Mix well so slices are evenly coated. Place in piecrust and dot with butter. Roll out top crust and gently place over filling. Crimp to seal edges, and make slits in the top crust for steam to escape. Bake at 425° for 60 minutes. Remove from oven and cool on a wire rack. I like to serve the pie slightly warm. This will serve 6.

Coffee Cinnamon Chocolate Chip Bars

Once I went to Seattle to celebrate my August birthday with friends, and found the weather so rainy and damp that candles were being lit in restaurants at lunchtime. In this cool city, with its gray weather, the coffee stands on every corner serve up the perfect beverage. Coffee is also popular for cooking there, and adds a heartening flavor to these delicious Northwest cookie bars.

⅓	cup butter or shortening, at room temperature
1	cup dark brown sugar
1	egg, beaten
½	cup strong coffee (cooled)
½	teaspoon baking soda
½	teaspoon baking powder
½	teaspoon salt
1⅔	cups flour
1	cup chocolate chips
½	cup coarsely chopped walnuts or peanuts

Cream butter and sugar together. Add egg and blend. Mix in coffee. Sift dry ingredients and add, mixing together until smooth. Fold in chips and nuts. Spread out evenly in a greased 9″ x 13″ pan. Bake at 375° for 20 minutes. Place pan on rack and cool. Cut into bars of desired size. These are lovely served with coffee ice cream and a steaming hot cup of coffee!

Rogue Valley Poached Pears

Oregon's Rogue River winds along for 215 miles before it finally meets the Pacific Ocean. This scenic river is popular for fishing, and Clark Gable and Zane Grey were both big fans of the Rogue. The valleys alongside the river, especially those near Medford, are famed for their pear orchards. One of the best local ways of preparing pears is this simple poaching. This dessert is very refreshing and most attractive.

- 4 ripe pears (Bartlett, Anjou, Comice, etc.)
- 1 lemon, juice and grated rind
- 1 cup sugar
- ½ teaspoon cinnamon
- 1 teaspoon vanilla
- 3 cups water
- for garnish: honey, toasted hazelnuts, or berries

Peel pears, leaving stem on. Combine lemon juice and rind, sugar, cinnamon, and vanilla with water. Add pears, stir, and bring to a simmer. Cook over a low flame for 8–10 minutes. The pears should be just barely tender, not mushy. You may need to roll them around during the cooking so all the pear is covered. Cool in the syrup. To serve, remove from syrup and place with stem up on plates. Drizzle honey over each pear and sprinkle with a few toasted, slivered hazelnuts. Sometimes, in Oregon, the pears are topped with berries that have been simmered with a little sugar for 3 minutes. This will serve 4.

Northwestern Drinks

Seattle Hot Cocoa

Hot cocoa is America's favorite childhood drink, which is not to say that adults, teenagers, and the elderly do not also enjoy cocoa. One of the most pleasant places in the nation to savor hot cocoa is a Seattle cafe overlooking the Puget Sound on a misty day.

- ¼ cup dry cocoa
- ½ cup sugar
- ½ cup water
- dash vanilla (optional)
- 1 quart milk
- marshmallows (optional)

Mix cocoa, sugar, and water together. Simmer for 3 minutes, stirring to blend. Slowly add milk. Stir and heat just until hot—do not boil. Serve to 6, topping each cup with marshmallows if desired. Sometimes a dab of whipped cream is added instead of marshmallows.

Oregon Celebration Raspberry Punch

Raspberries grow abundantly in Oregon's climate. This punch is popular for weddings and other celebrations.

- 1–2 cups fresh raspberries or 1 10-ounce package frozen
- 1 fifth dry white wine, chilled
- 1 bottle champagne, chilled

Wash fresh raspberries gently and pat dry. If frozen, thaw. Combine with champagne and wine in a glass punchbowl. This will serve 6–8.

Bloody Mary

While Bloody Marys are popular nationwide, they certainly are enjoyed in rustic Alaskan bars. Perhaps because this state is close to Russia, vodka seems to be a favored liquor.

1½	ounces vodka
3	ounces tomato juice
½	teaspoon Worcestershire sauce
	dash lemon juice
	dash celery salt
1	celery stalk for garnish (optional)

Shake ingredients together. Serve in a 6-ounce old-fashioned cocktail glass. Add an ice cube and a stalk of celery, if desired. This will make one Bloody Mary.

Kenai Campfire Coffee

Once we camped with our friends in their RV on the Alaskan Kenai Peninsula for a salmon fishing trip. In the evening, we made a big campfire and pulled up folding chairs around it. Neighboring campers came over to enjoy sitting by the fire and conversing together. D. D. made coffee. He and Gordon had been Marine buddies in World War II. They were veteran campfire coffee makers. Everyone agreed it was the best!

1	cup ground coffee (1½ cups for stronger coffee)
12	cups cold water plus 1 cup to settle grounds
2–3	eggshells (save from breakfast)

Mix coffee and water together. Place over campfire grill. Bring to a boil. Let simmer 4–5 minutes. Add cold water and eggshells to settle grounds. Let stand a minute before pouring. This will make 12 cups.

THE SOUTHWEST

The Southwest is a realm of rosy-orange canyons dotted with aromatic pinon trees. The scenery is dramatic, with sprawling deserts, high cliffs bearing ancient cave dwellings, and long vista views. The summers are torrid and the winters are very cold. This section of America is the domain of vast ranches famous for their cattle, cowboys, and master barbecue cooks. The crystalline air reveals sharp imagery in the endless landscape.

In Arizona, the Superstition Mountains rise from the flat desert and offer legends of hidden gold. In New Mexico, strings of red chiles (called *ristras*) dry in the autumn sun. The yellow rose of Texas blooms in gardens bordering the state's historic sites, and is even placed in a vase on my hotel bedside table. I have stood in the Alamo with other tourists and become teary-eyed as guides related the story of the heroic battle. Our family has camped under quaking aspens at the rim of the Grand Canyon, a wonder of nature that strikes awe in visitors from near and far. Once I watched hang gliders slowly and gracefully descend from the Sandia Mountains. Red hawks were following and soaring around them. In Santa Fe, I heard an opera under a chilly star-studded sky with flashes of lightning flitting across the Sangre de Cristo Mountain range. I have been a passenger in a tiny Cessna airplane, landing in Taos as the round blazing sun was dissolving into the skyline. With our pilot friends, we went to an adobe-style hotel. In our rooms, a beehive-shaped fireplace, glowing with a pinon log fire, gave a pleasant warmth. In a cozy nearby cafe, we all ate New Mexico stacked enchiladas and felt contented.

Culture is abundant in the Southwest, with famed potters, Kachina dancers, eminent jewelers who create masterpieces with silver and turquoise, talented weavers, storytellers, music and art festivals, and creative cooks. The Southwest has many treasures for its visitors.

Our Southwest is the birthplace of corn, beans, peppers, and squash. They are known as the "sacred sisters" and are the foundation of the region's cuisine. Corn represents the cycle of life, and is sacred to the past and present. The *milpa* system is still used for farming: The corn grows tall, the beans climb up the corn for support, and the squash and peppers flourish on the ground below. Because of its eclectic fusion of Spanish, Native American, and Mexican influences, Southwestern cooking is a colorful and distinct style of American cuisine.

Georgia O'Keeffe Watercress Soup

In the small town of Abiquiu, in northern New Mexico, Georgia O'Keeffe lived and painted many of her famous desert landscape works, inspired by the dramatic mountains, rocks, and sky of the surrounding countryside. O'Keeffe's cooking was simple and earthy, in keeping with her character, and she enjoyed watercress soup. Here is a version I think this great American woman might have liked very much.

- 1 pound white rose or red potatoes, peeled and sliced
- 4 cups water
- 1 medium white onion, peeled and diced
- salt and pepper to taste
- 1 bunch watercress
- 1 cup milk or half-and-half
- ¼ cup dry white wine (optional)

Place the potatoes, water, onion, salt, and pepper in a soup pot. Cover and simmer for about 40 minutes until the potatoes are very tender. Remove from heat and break up potatoes with a fork or potato masher, just until they are crumbly (do not use a blender or food processor, as you do not want a "mush"). Remove and discard about one inch of the watercress stems. Wash well. Cut across the bunch of watercress with a knife or scissors into 1-inch lengths. Add to soup and cook over low flame for 5 minutes. Add milk and wine if used. Stir to blend and heat just to serving temperature. Do not boil. This will serve 5. (On one of those blistering New Mexico summer days, Georgia might have preferred this soup cold. To serve it that way, simply cool soup and refrigerate; stir before serving.)

Santa Fe Gazpacho

Santa Fe was founded on the ruins of a native Indian village in 1610 as the Spanish capital of "New Mexico." In 1821, it came under Mexican rule, and finally under the American flag in 1912. The city's culinary heritage has many reminders of its Spanish past. Many of Santa Fe's colorful restaurants feature gazpacho, a cold soup originally from Spain, as a cooling prelude to dining. Green chiles and corn chips add a local touch. Please do not try to make this soup unless you have fresh tomatoes—it is a summertime soup!

4	large slices dense, good-quality white bread (3–4 cups)
3	pounds fresh ripe tomatoes, peeled and seeded
	half a medium cucumber
1	green or red bell pepper
1	4-ounce can diced green chiles (or ½ cup chopped fresh Anaheim chiles)
2	garlic cloves, crushed
4	cups water
3	tablespoons wine vinegar
	salt and pepper to taste
⅓	cup olive oil
1	cup crushed tortilla chips for garnish

Cut the bread, tomatoes, cucumber, and bell pepper into small pieces. Add chiles, garlic, water, vinegar, salt, and pepper. Place in a bowl, stir together, and leave to marinate at room temperature for one hour. Then carefully pour the mixture into a blender or food processor. Blend until smooth. Add the olive oil and blend an additional minute. Pour into a bowl, and add a few ice cubes. Store in refrigerator until needed (this will stay fresh, if refrigerated, for 3 days). Serve in individual bowls, garnishing with the chips. This will serve 6 generously.

Tortilla Soup

Tortilla soup is the star of Southwestern soups. It can be used as a beginning to a dinner, or served in a large portion as a complete meal in itself.

2	cups slivered cooked chicken breast
2–3	tablespoons vegetable oil
3	corn tortillas, cut in ¼-inch strips
¼	cup chopped onion
1	clove fresh garlic, minced
1	quart homemade or canned chicken broth
1	cup peeled tomatoes, diced (fresh or canned)
1	teaspoon cumin
	salt and pepper to taste
	juice of one lime (2 tablespoons)

Garnishes

1	ripe, peeled, diced avocado
¼	cup grated Jack or cheddar cheese
¼	cup coarsely chopped fresh cilantro

Fry tortilla strips in oil until crisp. Drain on paper towels and set aside. In same pan, lightly fry the onion and garlic just until limp. In a soup pot, heat the chicken broth; add onion, garlic, tomatoes, cumin, salt and pepper, and chicken. Simmer for 10 minutes. Stir in lime juice. Serve to 4 in soup bowls, sprinkling with the crisp tortilla strips and garnishes divided among the bowls.

New Mexico Albondigas Soup

Albondigas simply means "little meatballs" in Spanish. In New Mexico, this soup is popular on nippy winter evenings. It is improved by preparing ahead of time so the flavors can mellow. Serve it with warm tortillas and a fresh green salad to make a good comforting dinner.

1	pound lean ground beef (or ½ pound each ground beef and pork)
1	tablespoon vegetable oil
1	medium onion, minced
1	clove garlic, minced
1	slice white bread
1	egg, slightly beaten
½	teaspoon oregano
½	cup white or yellow cornmeal
1	fresh green Anaheim chile, chopped finely, (or ¼ cup canned, diced)
	salt and pepper to taste
1	quart chicken or beef stock (homemade or canned)
1	8-ounce can tomato sauce

Heat oil in a frying pan. Lightly brown the onion and garlic. Crumble the bread into the beaten egg. Mix together. Add to meat along with onion, garlic, oregano, cornmeal, chile, salt, and pepper. Make this mixture into meatballs about the size of a walnut.

Heat the stock with the tomato sauce. Drop the meatballs into the soup and simmer, uncovered, for 25 minutes. To serve, place 3 meatballs in each soup bowl. This will make 6 servings. If any albondigas are left over, they make good sandwiches.

Party Posole

In the Southwest, where *posole* is traditionally served at New Year's parties, it is said to bring good luck for the year. Posole can easily be made in large quantities, so it is an ideal "one pot" choice. Once while visiting Albuquerque with friends, we were invited to spend the night in an ancient adobe near the Sangre de Cristo Mountains. The occupants of this rustic dwelling were sort of hippies. My friend (who was once their caring high school teacher) had kept in touch with her former students, who eked out a bare existence by farming in this beautiful dramatic setting. There was posole cooking on their wood stove when we arrived. It was my first introduction to this New Mexico classic, and I devoured several bowls.

We slept on the floor. The crude outhouse was several hundred yards away, down a trail that had a big rooster dashing around to defend his territory. On the way down the trail at night, the New Mexico sky was an inky expanse overhead, spangled with bright stars.

This recipe will serve 2 for a cozy supper and may easily be enlarged for a party.

- 1 tablespoon lard or oil
- 1 pound pork (boneless shoulder), cut in small cubes
- 1 medium onion, peeled and coarsely chopped
- 2 garlic cloves, peeled and minced
- 1 15-ounce can yellow or white hominy
- salt and pepper to taste
- 1 4-ounce can diced green chile
- 1 teaspoon dried oregano
- 1 cup stock or water
- lime wedges and fresh cilantro for garnish

In a 2-quart soup pot, melt the lard. Fry pork, onion, and garlic until lightly browned. Add hominy (include liquid in can), salt, pepper, chiles, oregano, and stock. Cover and simmer for one hour, stirring now and then. Serve in soup bowls with warm tortillas. Garnish with lime wedges (they are squeezed into the posole) and cilantro. The recipe can be enlarged for parties and made the day ahead if desired.

Taos Enchiladas

When I first visited Taos, my friends took me to an atmospheric New Mexico restaurant. The room had a low, beamed ceiling, and colorful Native American rugs hung on the walls. I watched the diners at a nearby table eating something that looked like stacks of tortillas. Our waitress explained that this interesting-looking dish was "New Mexico style enchiladas." As a Californian, I had only experienced rolled enchiladas, so of course I had to try these. I finished every last bite, and these enchiladas have become one of my very favorite foods. The portions in this recipe can be varied. There are some men (at least in New Mexico!) who can very easily eat an entire stack of 12.

- 12 fresh corn tortillas
- 1½ cups grated cheddar or Jack cheese
- 4 fried eggs
- shortening or lard for frying
- chili sauce (from recipe below, or a 28-ounce can of Las Palmas red chili sauce)

Chili Sauce

- 2 tablespoons shortening
- 1 tablespoon flour
- 1 28-ounce can tomato puree
- 4 tablespoons chili powder
- 1 teaspoon salt

To make the chili sauce: Melt the shortening. Stir in the flour, blend, and brown slightly. Slowly stir in the tomato puree and chili powder. Cook over a low flame, stirring a few times, for 20 minutes. Set aside.

To prepare the enchiladas, melt about 1 tablespoon shortening in a frying pan. Lightly cook the tortillas on each side, adding more shortening as necessary. The idea is just to make the tortilla pliable. You do not need a ton of shortening; just a dab will do.

Take a baking pan or large platter that will fit 4 stacks of tortillas and place four tortillas side by side. Dribble some sauce, followed by cheese, on top of the tortillas. Repeat same procedure, including the top tortilla. Place in a 350° oven for 10 minutes. This may seem a short time, but longer cooking will make them mushy and the tortillas will lose their identity. Fry four eggs sunnyside up just before the enchiladas are finished. Top each stack with a fried egg. In New Mexico, a dish of finely chopped onions is served to sprinkle over the stacked enchiladas.

San Antonio River Walk Enchiladas

Of the many American "restaurant rows," the River Walk in the historic city of San Antonio is certainly one of the most unique. Lush tropical plants line the two-and-half-mile walk. Sightseeing boats wind up and down the gentle river. It is sort of an American version of Venice. After years of devastating floods, the city decided to pave over the river and turn it into an underground sewer. A group of devoted Texas ladies, who had a vision that this area could be turned into a beautiful, relaxing recreational space, waged a vigorous campaign to save the "Paseo del Rio." Under President Roosevelt, the WPA was enlisted for the construction of bridges and paths. The women's vision and steadfastness paid off, and today this walk is famous around the world. The restaurants that line the path are inviting; one can stroll and view menus and diners before selecting a dining spot. Many feature a special style of Tex-Mex cuisine with a Spanish influence. Their menus offer many versions of enchiladas. I especially enjoyed this version, prepared with fresh Gulf shrimp.

- 6 large flour tortillas
- 1 pound cooked shrimp (peeled, deveined, and tails removed)
- juice of one fresh lime (about 2 tablespoons)
- ½ teaspoon liquid smoke
- salt and pepper to taste
- 1 cup grated Jack cheese
- 1 cup sour cream
- 2 tablespoons diced fresh or canned green chiles
- 2 green onions, minced

Topping

- 1 cup sour cream
- 1 cup Jack cheese
- fresh cilantro for top garnish (about 2 tablespoons snipped in small pieces)

In a stainless steel or glass bowl combine the lime and liquid smoke. You may buy cooked shrimp or cook your own by simmering fresh shrimp in 1 quart of salted boiling water, uncovered, until shrimp turn pink—about 8 minutes. Place shrimp in the bowl and stir around so shrimp are covered with flavorings. Refrigerate to marinate at least one hour, or up to 12 hours.

Combine one cup cheese with one cup sour cream, the green onions, and the chiles. Add shrimp with flavorings. Do not drain. This is your filling. To fill flour tortillas, warm each tortilla in a heated iron frying pan until pliable. Divide filling into 6 portions. Place filling in center of tortilla and roll up. It will look like a tube. Place seam side down in a lightly greased baking dish. Combine topping ingredients (except cilantro) and spoon over top. Bake at 350° for 25 minutes. Sprinkle with cilantro. This will make 3 servings. In San Antonio, enchiladas are typically served with refried or black beans and rice.

Texas Chili

The dying words of the American frontier hero Kit Carson were reputedly "Wish I had time for one more bowl of chili!" Affectionately known as "a bowl of red," chili is a uniquely American dish.

The Texas town of Terlingua is famed worldwide for its serious chili contests. Although I have not entered my own chili recipe there, I have been a judge at local chili cook-offs. This is fun, but I approach it with caution. Once I had to taste 16 samples. Usually, chili scores are judged from one to ten, and often there is a tie and it must be retasted. Chili should look appetizing, and should have a pleasant aroma that appeals to your taste buds. First I look at the chili, which should be served in a sturdy white china bowl. If the chili appears gray and greasy I immediately give it low marks. The next step is to take a spoonful and slowly roll it around your mouth. This is to capture the flavors before swallowing. Chili texture is important. It should not be soupy. After each taste, I drink a swig of beer to clean my palate. Beer works better for this than soda crackers or bread! In serious contests, ground meat is never used, although it is the main ingredient in "Texas jailhouse chili." Jails in Texas began serving chili to their prisoners in the late 1800s as a way to use inexpensive cuts of meat. The Dallas County jail in the '30s still holds the reputation for the best jailhouse chili ever made.

I have used the following basic recipe for my cooking classes. Individual chili chefs can add more or less of the various ingredients according to their desires.

2–3	tablespoons oil or lard
1	onion, chopped
1	clove garlic, minced
1	jalapeño pepper, finely chopped (optional)
2	pounds beef (boneless chuck or round steak) or boneless pork shoulder, cut into ½-inch cubes
2	tablespoons chili powder
1	teaspoon dried oregano (optional)
	salt and pepper to taste
1	tablespoon ground cumin
1	cup liquid (beer, red wine, tequila, broth, etc.)
1	28-ounce can diced or crushed tomatoes
1	4-ounce can diced green chiles

Heat the oil or lard in a stew pot. Lightly brown the onion, garlic, and pepper. Remove from pot with a slotted spoon and set aside. Place the meat, chili powder, oregano, salt, pepper, and cumin into pot, and brown lightly, adding more oil if necessary. Return onion, garlic, and pepper to pan, along with the liquid, tomatoes, and green chiles. Cover and cook over a low flame for 1 hour and 15 minutes, until the meat is tender, stirring now and then. Serve in bowls to 4. This recipe may be enlarged for a chili party. If desired, serve with bowls of grated Jack or cheddar cheese, minced onions, sour cream, finely chopped red or green chiles, olives, or snipped cilantro. The chili's flavors will mellow if it is made a day ahead.

Texas Chicken-fried Steak

A friend of mine asked if chicken-fried steak was just fried chicken. For people who do not live in the South, this is certainly a valid question. This dish, a sort of Southern cult food, originated with the early Texas cowboys. The Longhorn steers they herded had only dry grass or cactus to graze on, which made the meat rather tough. Chuckwagon cooks found that if they pounded the meat with a mallet it made the steaks tender. Of course, frying is a pet method of Southern cooking, so the steaks were dipped in a batter and fried. The classic plate will include mashed potatoes with cream gravy. Chicken-fried steak is also served at Texas breakfasts, along with fried eggs, ranch fries, and biscuits covered with cream gravy. Personally, I like this kind of food. It makes you feel cozy and comfortably full.

1	pound top round steak, about ½ inch thick (or "cubed" steak)
2	eggs, beaten
	salt and pepper to taste
1	cup flour, plus 2 tablespoons for gravy
	oil or shortening for frying
1½	cups milk

Cut meat into 4 serving pieces and trim away any fat. Pound meat with a mallet until the meat is ¼ inch thick. Cube steaks may be used instead. Place the beaten eggs in a shallow bowl, and spread out the flour on waxed paper. Dip the meat in the flour, then in the egg, and once more in the flour. Set aside. Heat oil ½ inch deep in a cast-iron frying pan. When the oil is hot, but not smoking (370°), place the steaks in the pan. Fry for about 5 minutes on each side. They should look crispy and golden brown. Remove and place on a warm platter. They may be laid on paper towels to absorb any excess fat. Drain all but 2 tablespoons fat from the pan. Add flour and blend around in the pan to gather pan scraps and juices. Slowly add the milk. Season to taste with salt and pepper. Usually, a generous amount of pepper is added to cream gravy. Spread gravy over steaks and serve with hot mashed potatoes. This will serve 2.

Santa Fe Jalapeño Cheese Muffins

When traveling, it is often a most pleasant experience to stay in a bed-and-breakfast home instead of a hotel. In Santa Fe, we spent several days in a historic Colonial Manor home, the Grant Corner Inn, while we enjoyed the many restaurants, the museums, and the summer outdoor opera. The Inn's generous breakfast is served on the front porch and large indoor dining room. Louise Stewart, the exuberant owner, offered to share the recipe for one of their special breakfast offerings. These delicious muffins are full of Southwestern flavors.

2½	cups yellow cornmeal (preferably stone ground)
½	cup flour
2	teaspoons baking powder
½	teaspoon baking soda
½	teaspoon salt
2	eggs
2	cups buttermilk
½	cup vegetable oil
2	fresh jalapeños, seeded and finely chopped
1	cup grated sharp cheddar cheese
1	cup fresh or frozen corn kernels

Preheat oven to 425°. In a medium mixing bowl, combine cornmeal, flour, baking powder, soda, and salt, stirring well. Set aside.

In a medium bowl, beat eggs with buttermilk and oil. Pour into dry ingredients, stirring just to moisten. Stir in jalapeños, cheese, and corn. Spoon into paper-lined muffin cups or a greased muffin tin, as preferred. Fill three-fourths full.

Bake at 425° for 15–18 minutes, or until lightly browned. This will make 16 to 24 muffins, depending on desired size of muffin.

Rio Hondo Autumn Pear Salad

A New Mexico autumn is made up of fall colors and crisp evenings. The pears that ripen in the valleys alongside the Rio Hondo during this season are famed for their intense flavor and creamy texture. This salad, with its Mexican-style nutty topping, is perfect for the season's radiant moods.

4	pears, ripe to the touch (but not squishy)
4	tablespoons olive oil
2	tablespoons fresh lemon juice
	romaine or butter lettuce leaves to set the pears on
	freshly ground black pepper to taste

Nut Mixture

- 1 cup pecans or walnut halves
- 2 tablespoons vanilla
- 2 teaspoons Kahlua
- 1 tablespoon chili powder
- 2 tablespoons sugar

Combine nut mixture ingredients and roast in oven at 300° for 20 minutes. Cool and reserve.

Core and slice the pears (do not peel) and mix with oil and lemon juice. This may be done ahead. Place the lettuce leaves on a plate. Arrange the pear slices in a fan-like design, sprinkle with nuts, and serve to 4.

Texas Ranch-style Dressing

Restaurants and salad buffets offer a choice of dressings, and usually one of them is "ranch." This tangy, creamy combination is sold in supermarkets, but making your own is simple. I especially like this dressing on crispy romaine lettuce.

- 2 cups mayonnaise
- 2 cups buttermilk
- 1 teaspoon white wine vinegar
-   salt and pepper to taste
- 2 peeled and minced garlic cloves
- 2 green onions (white and green) cut in tiny pieces
- 2 tablespoons fresh minced parsley (optional)

Combine all ingredients and stir (a fork works well) until well blended. Refrigerate until needed. This will make one quart.

San Antonio Pecan Pie

Native Americans used the pecan for centuries before French missionaries "discovered" it in Illinois in the late 1600s. The pecans grown in the orchards around San Antonio are famed for their high quality, and this is one of the pecan growers' favorite recipes. Indeed, there are many who believe that the American Thanksgiving table is not complete without a sweet, translucent pecan pie. The version we make today was made possible by the introduction of corn syrup around 1900.

	one 9- or 10-inch piecrust*
3	eggs
⅔	cup dark or light brown sugar
1	cup dark or light corn syrup
⅓	cup butter, melted and slightly cooled
1	tablespoon vanilla
1	tablespoon bourbon, whiskey, or rum
1½	cups pecan halves
	whipped cream or ice cream for topping (optional)

Break eggs into a mixing bowl and with a whisk or electric beater mix until light and foamy. Add sugar. Pour in corn syrup, followed by butter and flavoring. Mix all together until blended. Stir in the pecan halves. Pour into pie shell and bake at 400° for 45 minutes. Some recipes use a lower temperature for baking, but I like the toasty flavor that comes from the higher heat. A knife inserted in the pie should come out clean when it's ready. Serve plain, or with desired topping, to 8. This pie is quite rich, so the slices should be of moderate size.

Canyon Road Spicy Crunch Cookies

Canyon Road in Santa Fe is lined with art galleries. It is, in fact, one of the largest concentrations of such galleries in America. One can spend hours wandering from gallery to gallery, viewing the best in Southwestern

---

*For basic piecrust recipe, see "Washington Apple Pie" in The Northwest and Alaska section. For a single crust, use one-half ingredient amounts.

THE SOUTHWEST

art, and new exhibits are always opening. These splendid cookies are popular at these artists' receptions, and go well with either wine or coffee.

- ½ pound butter, at room temperature
- ½ cup confectioners sugar
- 1 tablespoons vanilla or rum
- 2 cups flour
- ½ teaspoon salt
- 1 teaspoon cinnamon
- ½ teaspoon nutmeg
- 1 cup finely chopped walnuts or pecans
- confectioners sugar for "dusting," about 1 to 1½ cups

Cream butter with sugar and vanilla (or rum) until light and fluffy. Sift flour, salt, and spices together. Add gradually to the sugar mixture, blending well. Mix in nuts and again blend well. This is a rather crumbly dough, and for easier handling it can be chilled for 30 minutes if desired.

Moisten your hands with a little water. Gather up the dough and form into little 1-inch balls. Bake at 375° on an ungreased cookie sheet for 10–12 minutes. You want them just set and light brown. While warm, roll in confectioners sugar. Place on cooling rack. When cool, sprinkle with additional powdered sugar.

Favorite Drinks for Hot Summers and Cold Winters

Margaritas

The darling of Southwestern drinks is the classic Mexican margarita. Many restaurants offer the double in big bubble glasses. Margaritas are very refreshing and perfect with Southwest Mexican food.

- lime wedge
- salt
- 1½ ounces tequila
- ¾ ounce orange liqueur (triple sec or other)
- 1½ tablespoons lime juice (fresh preferred)
- crushed ice

Take the lime wedge and rub around the rim of a medium-sized glass or goblet. Place a layer of salt on a saucer. Rub the rim in salt to coat edge. Combine tequila, orange liqueur, and lime juice. Mix well. Add ice. Mix or shake to combine ingredients. Pour into glass. This will make one margarita.

White Sangria

This variation of sangria is very cooling for those torrid Southwestern summer days. The flavors are lovely and the appearance of summer's seasonal fruits floating in white wine is most attractive.

- 3 cups (about) sliced fruits of your choice: peaches, honeydew melon slices, apples, etc.
- 1 lemon, unpeeled, cut in thin slices
- 1 orange, unpeeled, cut in thin slices
- ½ cup sugar
- 1 bottle (750 ml) dry white wine
- 1 6-ounce bottle club soda

Combine fruit with sugar and wine. Cover and refrigerate at least an hour, or up to 12 hours. To serve, add the club soda to the wine and fruit mixture. Place in a pitcher with ice cubes. This will serve 4–5.

Texas Iced Tea

This is the most popular beverage in Texas homes, restaurants, and small cafes. It quenches thirst and is most refreshing.

- 1½ teaspoons tea (your choice) to each cup of water
- sugar to taste
- lemon slices
- mint sprigs (optional)

Prepare in a teapot by pouring boiling water over the tea. Cover and let steep for 3–5 minutes. Pour through strainer into pitcher. Add sugar and stir to mix. Refrigerate until needed. Serve in tall glasses over ice cubes, with lemon slices and a sprig of mint if desired.

THE WEST

The American West was settled by wagon trains, horses, mules, railways, and walkers. Sturdy individuals came out to the far West for sun, health, gold, and adventure, and the beauty and bounty of this region continue to beckon and allure. Westerners are determined and courageous citizens who continue to crusade to preserve their cherished land and freedom of spirit. The West contains many of the nation's national parks: Yosemite, Grand Canyon, Zion, Bryce, and Yellowstone. This part of the country is ravishingly beautiful.

I am a daughter of the West simply because my family on both sides came West in search of a happy and prosperous life. My Nana and Grandpa moved from New York City to Pasadena to open a piano school and raise their four children. My father's grandparents came from Utah to the pastoral northern California town of San Rafael to have a life in the West. Daddy left home at 16 to attend Occidental College, where he met my mother (living in nearby Pasadena) on a blind date. As a result, I began my life in a cottage home in Pasadena's Arroyo Seco.

During my California childhood, all the treasures of the state's diverse ethnic foods were mine to experience. I ate Mexican, Chinese, Japanese, Spanish, Korean, French, soul food, and Italian dishes, and curious ethnic variations in my young years. Abalone, artichokes, tangerines, avocados, egg rolls, and tortillas were all part of my menu.

Chefs and writers working in the West have created a unique style of cooking. These resourceful individuals are filled with unrestrained creative power. Alice Waters, Wolfgang Puck, Jeremiah Tower, and the American darling, Julia Child, along with the late

M.F.K. Fisher, James Beard, and Helen Evans Brown, are all a part of our Western cooking legacy.

Western hospitality and fondness for parties have long been famed throughout the country. Fiestas, festivals, and celebrations on ranches and farms and in cities could last for days in the early times of the West. There is an overt friendliness that is characteristic of this region. Because of the Western states' pleasant climate, picnics and home barbecues are favorite social events. An appreciation of both fine and simple dining and food belong to the West.

Celery Victor

Victor Hirtzler was a renowned chef many decades ago at the Saint Francis Hotel in San Francisco, where he created this dish for the famous patrons of the hotel dining room. It has remained a California classic and is a light and flavorful accompaniment for any occasion.

- 1 medium bunch celery
- 3 cups chicken broth, homemade or canned
- 1 cup French dressing
- fresh red pepper or pimiento for garnish
- salt and freshly ground pepper

Basic French Dressing

- ⅔ cup olive oil
- ⅓ cup wine vinegar
- salt and pepper to taste

Trim the celery; wash and cut the choice center sections into 5-inch stalks. Place stalks in a saucepan and cover with chicken broth. Simmer, covered, just until tender, about 30 minutes. Cool in the broth. Remove the celery from the broth, draining well. Save this delicious celery-flavored broth for a foggy day's lunch.

Place the celery in the dressing and chill for several hours or even overnight. To serve, remove celery from the dressing. Place 3 stalks on a small serving plate, spoon some of the dressing on top, and garnish with the pepper or pimiento made into an "X" design. Celery Victor will taste even better if you let it stand out of the refrigerator for 15 or 20 minutes. Overchilling foods dulls their flavor. Sometimes anchovies are used in place of peppers, and sometimes crab legs, slices of hard-boiled egg, or tomato slices are added. Chef Hirtzler liked to use white wine vinegar in his French dressing for this dish.

San Pedro Marinated Vegetables

San Pedro is one of Southern California's busiest ports. Big ships arrive and depart as sailboats drift in and out. In the colorful hilly streets, there are seamen's homes for sailors from many nations. The population is very diverse, and a large part of the city's culture is Italian. My friends and I love to go on food-shopping adventures in San Pedro, where one of our favorite stops is an Italian delicatessen. Many ships buy their provisions from this popular spot, so it is always lively and crowded. The exuberant male employees flirt with the lady customers and tell them how beautiful they are. One of the specialties in the food cases of this and other Italian-American delis is the marinated vegetables. These are easy to make in your own kitchen and certainly provide a wonderful beginning or accompaniment to any dinner.

1	6-ounce can black or green pitted olives, *OR*
1	pound fresh mushrooms, *OR*
1	pound fresh sliced zucchini
1	garlic clove, peeled and minced
1	teaspoon dried red pepper flakes
½	teaspoon oregano (optional)
	salt and pepper to taste
½	cup olive oil
3	tablespoons red or white vinegar

This is a casual recipe that can be enlarged to include as many additional vegetables as you like. After the vegetables are drained, the marinade can be used for a salad dressing—all of that flavor should not be wasted.

If olives are used, drain them. Mix marinade ingredients in a jar or bowl and stir well with a fork to blend. Add olives. If mushrooms are used, gently brush off any dirt, remove the stems and add to marinade. If zucchini is used, simply wash and cut into long slivers before placing in marinade. Stir so the vegetables are completely coated, and refrigerate at least 4 hours or overnight. To serve, remove from the refrigerator and let sit at room temperature for about 20 minutes for the oil to liquefy. Drain and place in a pretty bowl.

Las Vegas Shrimp Cocktail

The first time I went to Las Vegas countless years ago, I was on the way to Utah to visit relatives. This was our overnight stay on the road to Salt Lake City. My husband and I both had Mormon great-grandfathers, and we have always been curious—could they have known each other? My relative was from Scotland and Gordon's from Wales.

It was almost dinnertime and we wandered into a casino. There was a food counter serving shrimp cocktails for only 10 cents. The pale pink shrimp were in little glass bowls covered with a reddish sauce. I ordered two cocktails. They were cool and refreshing after the warm, monotonous drive. It occurred to me that it was a rather remarkable experience to nibble these pretty gems from the sea in the very midst of a dry Nevada desert. The curious city of Las Vegas is an American novelty, and shrimp cocktails have been a traditional food offering here almost since the city's founding. Shrimp cocktails are not only popular in Las Vegas; almost every restaurant menu in our country has a place for shrimp cocktail.

- 1 pound cooked and peeled shrimp, chilled
- 3 tablespoons lemon juice

Cocktail Sauce

- ¾ cup chili sauce
- ½ cup ketchup
- 1 tablespoon finely minced onion (chives may be used)
- 1 tablespoon horseradish
- 2 tablespoons finely minced fresh celery
- salt and pepper to taste

Mix shrimp and lemon juice together in a bowl and refrigerate. Place all the sauce ingredients in another bowl, blend, and refrigerate. To serve, place shrimp and lemon juice in 4 bowls (for small cocktails). Dribble sauce over top and serve at once.

Sonoma Spinach-filled Hard-boiled Eggs

Sonoma is a historic town in California's wine country. In the center of the city are a mission and plaza with large trees and bronze sculptures. It is a perfect spot for a picnic, and often there are festivals here to celebrate various events. The plaza fills with crafts, food, and wine-tasting tables, all to help some favorite charity. At one of these events, I sampled this Northern Italian dish from one of the local vineyards' Italian-American owners. The eggs were presented on a large platter lined with fresh grape leaves. Eggs and spinach are a superb combination.

12	eggs, hard-boiled
1	10-ounce package frozen chopped spinach (or 1 bunch fresh, cooked and chopped)
¼	cup mayonnaise
2	tablespoons olive oil
2	tablespoons Parmesan cheese
	salt and pepper to taste

Cook the spinach. Drain and squeeze dry. This step is very important, as excess spinach juice will dilute the filling. Carefully shell the eggs. Cut in half. Separate yolks from whites. Mash yolks with spinach, mayonnaise, oil, cheese, salt, and pepper. Carefully fill each egg white half with the yolk mixture. You want the filling in the center and not dribbling over the sides, to create a pristine appearance of the yellow-green against the white. Chill, covered with plastic wrap or foil, until needed. This can be made up to 2 days ahead.

Yellow Squash Soup with M.F.K. Fisher

After I had corresponded for some years with the famed food writer Mary Frances Kennedy Fisher, whom I idolized, a letter arrived inviting me and my husband to visit her. The date she had chosen happened to be my birthday, August 5th!

That morning, I called her from the small northern California town of Glenn Ellen, where she lived. It did seem like good manners to reconfirm our visit. The voice that answered sounded like a young girl. I worried that I might have dialed the wrong number, but she said, "This is Mary Frances and I am looking forward to meeting you."

Her "last house" (she never wanted to move again) is located on the Bouvrie Ranch, a quick turn off Highway 41. Beside the door of the small white stuccoed house hung a weathered little mission bell. I pulled the string and, like magic, the door was opened by a tall and very real Mary Frances. Bright lipstick painted her cupid's-bow lips, and her eyebrows were perfectly penciled. Dressed casually in light green velour, she welcomed us warmly, offering us wine and a bowl of almonds. Suddenly it seemed like we were special friends. This was our first meeting, the beginning of many until her death in 1994.

We shared many common interests. Timmy (her second husband and the love of her life) had been an artist like my Gordon. We all had a passion for France. Mary Frances' special appeal for me as a friend was her basic, unabashed honesty and straightforward thoughts on any subject. She loved to help others with their works, and her interest in us and our family was touching.

One nostalgic memory I have of her is of a time when I was working on a California Wine Country cookbook. Mary Frances was interested in the project and had been sharing some of her thoughts with me. She invited us for lunch to talk about the book. It was a late autumn day that had turned chilly. The wind was blowing, and dark clouds flitted across the sky. We came into her cozy front room, where a fire burned in the fireplace. (The ranch supplied Mary Frances with downed oak and madrona wood, and she enjoyed the ritual of preparing a fire.) A tray with a wine bottle and glasses was waiting for us. On the sill of a window that looked out across to the Sonoma Mountains, there were flowering early red tulips. After an exchange of our latest news, I was asked to stir the soup while Mary Frances prepared the rest of our lunch. She explained that the soup was made of yellow squash, the gift of a vegetable gardener friend. The soup was ladled into green earthenware bowls. On the table were fresh wheat bread (from another friend), goat cheese, and a small tray of smoked Oregon salmon. We all drank some Pinot Noir Blanc, a favorite of hers. Dessert was ice cream with a blueberry sauce dribbled over the top and ginger cookies. I never had a precise recipe for Mary Frances' soup, however, this is as I remember it was made.

1	pound yellow crookneck or straightnut squash
2	tablespoons butter
1	cup chopped white onion
2	cups chicken broth
2	tablespoons dry white wine (optional)
	salt and pepper to taste
	plain yogurt for topping
	sprinkle of paprika

Wash and cut squash into ½-inch pieces. Cover with salted water and cook covered just until tender, about 8 minutes. Drain and set aside. Heat the butter in a small frying pan. Fry the onion until just limp, but not brown. Combine onion with squash, broth, wine, salt and pepper. Place in a blender or food processor and blend until smooth. Heat and serve with topping of yogurt dusted with paprika. This will make 4 medium-sized bowls.

Fisherman's Wharf Cioppino

Tourists and local residents both love Fisherman's Wharf in San Francisco. They enjoy the historic ships, dining in the many restaurants, or just strolling along, nibbling on a take-out shrimp or crab cocktail. Everyone always seems to be having a great time.

During the 1920s, San Francisco was a major fishing port, and Fisherman's Wharf was jammed with fishing boats. While the fishermen were sorting out the day's catch, it was traditional to prepare a fish soup on the ship's deck. Accounts from those days report that tantalizing smells filled the wharf. The word *cioppino* reputedly originated from the cry "Chip in, o!" The men would add whatever was in their bounty to the simmering pot. This is still the best method to prepare this soup, just using what is fresh and in season. Use this recipe simply as a basic guideline for cioppino.

Despite its humble origins, cioppino makes a superb company dinner. Guests can serve themselves from the soup pot, and fresh sourdough bread is provided for wiping up the flavorful juices. Red wine and big napkins should be included.

¼	cup olive oil
1	medium onion, chopped
1	green pepper, chopped
2	fresh garlic cloves, minced
2	cups red or white wine
	salt and pepper to taste
1	bay leaf
½	teaspoon thyme
2	28-ounce cans diced or crushed tomatoes
1	pound halibut or other firm white fish, cut in 1-inch cubes
12	small fresh clams in the shell, scrubbed (or one 6½-ounce can chopped clams)
½	pound scallops or fresh crab
	fresh minced parsley for garnish

In a large soup pot, heat the olive oil over a medium flame. Add the onion, pepper, and garlic. Stir and cook just until limp. Add wine, seasonings, and tomatoes. Mix together and simmer, uncovered, over a low flame for 30 minutes. (This much may be done ahead, and the stock refrigerated until ready for use.)

Add the halibut and clams to the simmering stock. Cook for 15 minutes, covered. Uncover, add scallops or crab, and continue to simmer for another 10 minutes. Garnish with parsley and serve from the pot. This will make 4 generous servings.

Idaho Rainbow Trout

Travel posters from Idaho always include a picture of a fisherman standing in a woodsy scenic setting, casting his fishing line in a rippling stream. It is true that scenes like this are to be found everywhere in Idaho. Many fishermen, including Ernest Hemingway, have come to lure away the trout from rivers and streams. If you have tasted freshly caught trout fried over a campfire, you know this is the very best; but the next best is trout from your local supermarket. Trout is a plentiful fish available in most markets all year, shipped fresh or frozen. It was quite a favorite of Franz Schubert, who composed a song and quartet about this lovely shimmering water creature, "Die Forelle."

4	fresh or frozen trout, about 8 ounces each, cleaned
	flour for dusting
	salt and pepper to taste
¼	cup cooking oil
½	cup butter
½	pound fresh mushrooms, sliced
	lemon wedges and parsley for garnish

Pat the trout dry. Dust with flour. Sprinkle with salt and pepper. Heat oil and half the butter (¼ cup) in a large, preferably iron, frying pan. When well heated, add the trout. Brown well on both sides, about 5 minutes on each side. Meanwhile, in another frying pan, melt the remaining ¼ cup butter over a medium flame. Gently fry the mushrooms with a sprinkling of salt and pepper just until light brown. Remove from heat.

When the trout is done, place on a warm serving platter and top with mushrooms. Garnish with the lemon and parsley. Traditionally, this is served with plain boiled potatoes. This will serve 4.

Zesty Catalina Swordfish

Santa Catalina is an island about 22 miles across the sea (as the song goes) from Los Angeles. The waters are very clear and perfect for swimming and snorkeling, making the island a vacation paradise for many. On the boat trip across the Catalina Channel to the island, one can see dolphins and flying fish, while deeper in the channel are swordfish, famed for their fine sharp flavor and firm texture. The island's historic casino contains the largest circular dance floor in America. We were fortunate to be guests for a wedding party in this glorious room, and Catalina swordfish was part of the sumptuous wedding buffet.

Swordfish, served with boiled red potatoes and spinach, makes a delicious dinner. There is so much flavor to this fish that it should not be disguised with sauces; the simplest ways of preparing it really are best. Please do not worry that frying fish might be unhealthful—frying seals in the flavor, and when drained the fat is insignificant.

2	swordfish steaks, about ¾ pound each, cut 1 inch thick (other firm fish such as sea bass or halibut may also be used)
2	tablespoons butter
2	tablespoons peanut oil (or other vegetable oil)
	salt and pepper to taste
2	teaspoons capers (optional)
¼	cup white wine
	lemon wedges

Pat the surface of the fish dry with paper towels. Removing excess moisture is very important for good frying. In a heavy frying pan that will fit the fish without crowding, heat the butter and oil until just sizzling, but not smoking. Place the swordfish in the pan and sprinkle it with salt and pepper. Fry for approximately 5 minutes. Turn over, adding additional equal amounts of butter and oil if pan should seem dry. Salt and pepper top surface. Cook until fish is done, about another 5 minutes (the fish is done when it flakes easily if gently probed with the tines of a fork). Remove to a warmed plate. Add wine and capers to the pan, swirl around to gather up pan juices for a minute, and pour over swordfish. Serve to 2 with a garnish of lemon wedges.

Rancho Days Fiesta Enchiladas

In California, schoolchildren always learn about the "rancho days," as the time of the great Spanish ranches is called. During this colorful period, almost any occasion was enough reason for a fiesta (party). It might be a roundup, birth, marriage, or harvest. The guests came on horseback from miles away, and the fiestas lasted several days, so the guests were given overnight accommodations. The music, feasting, and dancing went on far into the night. Barbecued meats were served, accompanied by large trays of enchiladas and beans. This "updated" enchilada is perfect for a party today.

12	medium flour or corn tortillas
2	whole cooked chicken breasts
1	8-ounce package cream cheese, at room temperature
6	green onions, minced
	salt and pepper to taste
1	4-ounce can diced green chiles
2	cups grated Jack cheese
1	cup sour cream
1	8-ounce can tomato sauce
1	teaspoon chili powder
	oil for frying, if corn tortillas are used
	cilantro and avocado slices for garnish (optional)

Prepare the chicken breasts by removing bone and skin. Shred the meat into long pieces. Mash the cream cheese with a spoon until smooth. Mix in chicken, green onions, salt, pepper, and one half of the diced chiles. Now mix in one cup of the Jack cheese. This is the filling for the enchiladas and may be prepared ahead. If flour tortillas are used, simply heat until limp in a frying pan. If you use corn tortillas, heat a little oil in a frying pan and fry each tortilla until limp, adding oil as needed.

Fill each tortilla with about 2 tablespoons of the filling. Roll the tortilla and place seam-side down in a lightly greased baking pan. Mix the sour cream with tomato sauce, chili powder, and remaining diced chiles. Spoon over tortillas. Sprinkle with remaining cheese. Bake uncovered for 20 minutes at 325°. They should be just hot, with the cheese melted (you do not want overcooked, mushy tortillas). Garnish as desired. Cilantro leaves and pale green avocado slices make a lovely topping.

Luisa Tetrazzini's Chicken and Pasta Casserole

Luisa Tetrazzini was a famous opera singer who made her debut in San Francisco and sang there every opera season. She loved this city, they loved her, and she gave lavish after-the-opera parties. This recipe was one of her creations. It is a very useful recipe for entertaining, as it is made ahead and heated while guests enjoy appetizers and wine. While there are many versions of it across the country, this recipe is the classic one.

½	pound (8 ounces) spaghettini
⅓	cup butter
3	tablespoons flour
2	cups half-and-half
	salt and pepper to taste
¼	teaspoon cayenne pepper (optional)
1	medium green bell pepper, chopped
¾	pound mushrooms, thinly sliced
3	cups diced and cooked boneless chicken breast or other parts
3	tablespoons sherry
1	cup grated Parmesan cheese
	minced parsley for garnish

Cook the spaghettini as per package directions to *al dente* firmness. Do not let it become mushy. Drain and set aside. Melt the butter in a saucepan. Blend in the flour and cook together for a minute. Slowly add the half-and-half, stirring until the mixture is slightly thickened (this is a thin sauce). Add the salt, pepper, and cayenne. Stir in the green pepper, mushrooms, chicken, and sherry. Blend well and set aside.

Lightly butter a 3-quart baking dish. Place the pasta on the bottom, and pour the chicken mixture on top. Sprinkle with the Parmesan. Cook uncovered in a 350° oven for 45 minutes. If you make Luisa's casserole ahead of time and refrigerate it, allow about 20 minutes extra for baking. Garnish it with minced parsley. This will serve 6 generously.

Les Guthrie's Mother's Meat Loaf

Les Guthrie is one of our closest friends. He went to Mount Vernon Junior High School in southwestern Los Angeles with Gordon. We all knew his mom, Elsie. She was a good cook! Les was especially fond of her meat loaf. Like many of our mothers she did not use an exact recipe, and like many of our mothers she is no longer with us to answer recipe questions. This has left Les to reconstruct the recipe to the best of his memory. I have retested it several times, and we both feel satisfied that Elsie would approve the recipe.

The virtues of this meat loaf are its flavor, the slightly crunchy texture, and the flecks of tomato adding to its appearance. It makes delicious sandwiches. I had so many meat loaves during the testing that I found other uses for it. One such use was as taco filling! Simply warm some meat loaf (the amount depends on the number of tacos; about ¼ cup meat per taco) and season with chili powder. It also can be turned into a spaghetti sauce (2 servings) by frying 2 minced garlic cloves and 1 chopped onion in 2 tablespoons olive oil; add one cup of the meat loaf, crumbled, and one 14-ounce can of diced tomatoes. Stir and simmer for 20 minutes. Serve on the pasta of your choice. In our research, we found that the loaf does not slice well when right out of the oven. It needs to stand about 20 minutes. Les remembers that his mom sometimes made it a day ahead, refrigerated the loaf, and reheated it the next day. This reheating will take about 25 minutes in a 350° oven, uncovered.

2	eggs
½	cup Worcestershire sauce
½	cup white wine or chicken broth
2	cups soft bread crumbs
1	14-ounce can peeled and diced tomatoes
⅓	cup Dijon mustard
	salt and pepper to taste (recommended: ⅛ teaspoon pepper and ¾ teaspoon salt)
1	cup finely chopped white or Spanish onion
1	cup finely diced celery
1½	pounds ground round steak (fat removed)
¾	pound lean ground pork

Beat eggs in a bowl, add Worcestershire sauce and wine or broth. Add crumbs and let them absorb the liquids for 10 minutes. Place remaining ingredients in a large bowl and mix well. I use my hands (washed beforehand, of course). Bake in two 5″ x 9″ x 3″ loaf pans for 1 hour and 15 minutes at 350°. Serve hot or cold. You can also freeze the extra loaf for future use. A note about the meat: Both Les' mother and my own always selected the meat and had the butcher grind it for them. We both recommend this procedure.

Los Angeles Tamale Pie

Tamale pie is a unique combination of Californian and Mexican flavors. This casserole has been a favorite of American cooks for many decades. It is a very good party main dish as it can easily be prepared ahead (for a party host or hostess, it is always advisable to avoid last-minute rushing around the kitchen!). Tamale pie is traditionally served with hot tortillas and a green salad. Cold beer is the perfect beverage for this Los Angeles supper.

Cornmeal Crust

- 5 cups water
- 1 tablespoon butter or olive oil
- 1 teaspoon salt
- 1 teaspoon chili powder
- 2½ cups cornmeal

Filling

- 1 tablespoon vegetable oil or bacon drippings
- 1 pound ground beef
- 1 tablespoon chili powder
- 1 teaspoon cumin (optional)
- salt to taste
- 1 medium onion, peeled and chopped
- 1 medium green or red bell pepper, chopped
- 1 28-ounce can diced or solid-pack tomatoes (or 2 cups fresh, chopped)
- 1 cup fresh corn (scraped from cob) or 1 cup canned or frozen

Topping

1   cup grated cheddar cheese
1   cup pitted, sliced black olives

To make the crust: Bring water to boil in a large pot, then reduce heat to simmer. Slowly pour in the cornmeal, seasonings, and butter or oil. Stir with a wooden spoon to blend. Continue cooking over a low flame for 15 minutes, stirring now and then to prevent mixture from sticking to the bottom. Set aside.

To make the filling: In a large frying pan, heat the oil, then add meat and seasonings. Stir around to blend. Add onion and green pepper. Fry until meat loses pink color. Now add tomatoes and corn. Some cooks like to add additional Anaheim chiles or diced green chiles, but this is up to your taste. Simmer for 20 minutes, stirring now and then.

To Assemble

Lightly grease a 2-quart shallow baking dish or casserole. Line with two-thirds of the cornmeal mixture. Add filling, and top with remaining crust. You may have to dip your hands in cold water and sort of pat this top crust around. Sprinkle with grated cheese and olives. Bake at 350° for 40 minutes. This will serve 6–8, depending on appetites.

America's Favorite: Hot Dogs

Like most Americans, I've had my favorite experiences with hot dogs at sporting events and Fourth of July barbecues. Our family always spent the Fourth with my father's college fraternity brother, Dick. He and his wife Eleanor lived in a sprawling house with a large backyard in San Marino, near Pasadena. Before we drove to their house, my dad would take my sister and me to a fireworks stand. He liked to buy rockets, and my sister and I liked sparklers, snakes, and "houses on fire." When we arrived, we could smell the barbecue smoke. Hamburgers and hot dogs were all ready to plop on the grill. There was bright yellow mustard and pickle relish for the hot dogs, and the buns were split, buttered, and toasted. If we wanted, we could add a slice of cheddar cheese. Eleanor made a creamy potato salad to go with the supper. Sometimes my dad and Dick attempted to make fresh strawberry ice cream in an old-time machine. It did not always work perfectly, but the result tasted good. As dusk descended, we began the fireworks show, lighting one thing at a time to lengthen the fun. If we were hungry again before we drove home, we could nibble on cold hot dogs which somehow tasted extraordinary.

Hot dogs also bring back memories of sporting events. My dad was a *Los Angeles Times* sports reporter. As part of his job, he covered various baseball, football, and basketball events. He had to stay until the very end because he had to record the final scores. Daddy enjoyed taking me with him, as we always had a good time together. I must admit sports were not my big interest, but I did have an interest in boys and it was entertaining to watch the various team members jump around in their athletic outfits. My dad would always get me one or two hot dogs to munch on while watching the action. Some stadiums had better ones than others. I did not like the hot dogs that arrived lukewarm, in soft buns that crumbled.

Hot dogs came to our country from Frankfurt with the German immigrants. During the St. Louis World's Fair in 1904, a clever food seller combined a roll with the Frankfurt-style wurst. A sports cartoonist created a drawing of a dachshund (its body the shape of a sausage) in a bun, and almost overnight the term "hot dog" became part of our American culinary language.

For One Hot Dog

- 1 good-quality hot dog bun (quality is important!)
- 1 hot dog of your choice
- butter (optional)
- your favorite mustard
- pickle relish (optional)
- other additions might be cheese, lettuce, or ketchup

There are many ways to prepare hot dogs. Some cooks just simmer them in boiling water until hot, about 8 minutes. They may be grilled on a barbecue. Sometimes a little oil is heated in an iron frying pan and the hot dog is fried on all sides. The timing is not exact, you just want your dog hot! When I was a Girl Scout, we pierced the dog with a fork and let it dangle over a campfire. Somehow, hot dogs always seem to taste best in the outdoors.

Chinese Eggs Foo Yung

Most towns in the United States have a Chinese restaurant these days. The Chinese were some of our first immigrants. Among them were many talented cooks, and their wonderful dishes have come to be a cherished part of America's menu. In the southwestern neighborhood of Los Angeles where I grew up, there was a cozy Chinese restaurant on the main street. I was always excited to go there to dinner with my family. My sister and I tried to eat with chopsticks and drank tea from pretty china cups. We both thought eggs foo yung was very foreign and tasty. It arrived on an oval white platter, with a shiny brownish sauce poured over the cakes. I like to make this at home for a light supper with steamed rice.

3	eggs
1	cup fresh bean sprouts
¼	cup minced pork, chicken, or shrimp (optional)
2	tablespoons minced green onion
1	tablespoon soy sauce
3–4	tablespoons peanut or salad oil

Sauce

1	cup chicken broth
1	tablespoon cornstarch
1	tablespoon soy sauce

Beat eggs in a bowl until slightly thick. Add the rest of the ingredients except oil, and blend. Do not prepare this ahead because it will get watery. This is a last-minute affair.

Heat oil in a frying pan. When oil is hot, pour about ¼ cup of the batter into the oil. Repeat the procedure until you have as many pancakes as your pan will hold without overcrowding. Cook a few minutes on one side; turn over and cook on the other. You may need an extra turn of the cakes to get the perfect doneness. They should be golden brown on each side. This will make about 8 pancakes.

To make the sauce, simply place the broth in a saucepan. Whisk in the cornstarch and soy sauce. Heat slowly while whisking until slightly thick. Place pancakes on a warm platter. Spoon sauce over the eggs foo yung.

Everyday Lunch Tuna Sandwiches

In most American workplaces, cafeterias, and homes, tuna sandwiches are a favorite for lunch. When I was on a tour of China, our whole busload of nearly 40 tourists started talking about tuna sandwiches. We had been eating only Chinese food for the last 10 days and somehow this subject seemed fun. By the time we arrived at the next sightseeing destination, everyone was hungry for a tuna sandwich. All the variations had been discussed. Some liked pickle relish, one liked a hard-boiled egg mashed with the tuna, another liked chopped celery, and there was one who always added capers. There is no doubt that Americans are passionate about tuna sandwiches!

- 4 slices bread, any sort (toasted if desired)
- 1 6-ounce can tuna (solid white is best)
- salt and pepper to taste
- 2–3 tablespoons mayonnaise
- options: 1 teaspoon lemon juice, 1 teaspoon pickle relish, 1 tablespoon grated apple, 1 tablespoon minced onion or chives, 2 tablespoons finely chopped celery, chopped hard-boiled egg, 1 tablespoon diced cucumbers, 1 tablespoon shredded iceberg lettuce, 1 teaspoon capers, etc.

Mix first four ingredients together with desired optional choices. Spread on bread and serve to 2. Somehow, potato chips are the perfect accompaniment for tuna sandwiches.

California Mission Days Green Chile Rice

The missions founded by Father Serra in Carmel in 1770 are some of the main tourist attractions of California. They stretched from San Diego to San Rafael, twenty-two of them in all. Today, most are open to visitors, with displays and exhibits on California mission life. Often, there are demonstrations of various crafts from mission times. All the missions had gardens for the produce needed to feed the many people who worked there.

Rice was one of the popular dishes in mission cuisine, and this blend of rice with green chiles is one of my favorite recipes. You can make a main dish of this classic by adding 1 to 2 cups cooked chicken pieces, bay shrimp, or shredded pork. It is a perfect "pot-luck" contribution and goes well as a side dish for barbecue dinners.

- 3 cups cooked rice (1 cup before cooking)
- 1 teaspoon chili powder
- 1 teaspoon cumin seed or cumin powder (optional)
- 1 teaspoon salt
- 2 cups sour cream
- 1 6-ounce can green chiles (or 4 fresh, peeled chiles), minced
- 2 cups grated Jack or cheddar cheese
- cilantro, tomato slices, or olives for garnish (optional)

Cook rice by your favorite method. Cool slightly. Add chili powder, cumin, and salt. Mix in sour cream and stir well. Lightly oil a 1½-quart baking dish. Place half the rice mixture, half the green chiles, and half the cheese in layers. Repeat, ending with the cheese. Bake in a 350° oven for 25 minutes, uncovered. Garnish if desired with fresh cilantro, sliced tomatoes, or a few sliced olives. This will serve 6.

San Francisco Stir-fried Asparagus

Chinese food is always a favorite at American tables, and nearly every town has at least one Chinese restaurant. In San Francisco's Chinatown, one can find cuisines from the many regions of China, offering so many choices for dining it becomes almost impossible to decide!

Most Chinese food is prepared in woks. These efficient pots are perfect for stir-frying asparagus, but a skillet can also be used. Cooking asparagus this easy way will give you a crisp, intensely flavored delight.

1	pound asparagus, washed
2	tablespoons peanut or other cooking oil
	salt and pepper to taste
2	tablespoons soy sauce

Take each stalk in your hand and bend. It will snap off naturally between the tender upper half and woody bottom stem. Save the bottom stems for soup. Lay the upper stems on a cutting board and cut them in 1-inch pieces, on a diagonal.

Heat oil in a large skillet or wok. Add the asparagus pieces and sprinkle with salt and pepper. Give a stir and cover. Shake the pan a few times as the asparagus is cooking. After two minutes, lift the lid and stir the stems around. Cover and repeat procedure for another 3 minutes. Uncover, add the soy sauce, and give a final stir. Of course, you can cook this uncovered, but by covering it you create a little steam, which makes the asparagus tender inside and crunchy outside. This will serve 3.

Idaho Perfect Baked Potatoes and Variations

When I first lived in Paris some decades ago, I was always craving a baked potato, and there were none to be found. The French were eating *pommes frites,* potatoes Anna, and soufflé potatoes; who had ever heard of *baked* potatoes?

Baked potatoes are truly an American specialty. While potatoes are grown in many states, it is Idaho that produces the very best baking potatoes. Recently, on a summer's evening, I had dinner at the American Harvest restaurant in New York's Rockefeller Center. It was a lovely warm evening. We sat in the outdoor patio under an umbrella. Three Frenchmen dining at a neighboring table were raving about the baked Idaho potatoes accompanying the steamed Maine lobster. They all agreed it was one of the finest American foods they had tasted. I had to order the same thing as I can never get my fill of baked potatoes.

Potatoes are very good for you, anyway. A 5-ounce potato has only 100 calories. It is full of vitamin C and fiber, high in minerals such as potassium, and low in sodium.

Wash the potatoes and cut a thin slice from each end. This is to prevent the potatoes from bursting in the oven, which is a MESS every cook wants to avoid. Lightly rub a small amount of oil all over the potato. This is to make the skin tender and attractive. Place the potato on a piece of foil on a baking sheet. Never wrap them in foil to bake, as this produces a potato that is steamed instead of baked. Bake at 425° for one hour or until tender (soft and pliable when you touch it). Using a potholder for this (the potato is hot!), remove from the oven and cut a big cross in the center of the potato. Push gently (being careful not to burn yourself) at each end so the potato will open up. Place your choice of topping in this cavity.

To make stuffed baked potatoes, carefully cut the baked potato in half. Remove insides with a spoon. Mix with butter and sour cream, and salt and pepper to taste. You will need about 3 tablespoons sour cream and 1 tablespoon butter per potato. Some people like them moist and some like them drier. Put the mixture back into the potato skins and place on baking sheets. Rebake in a 400° oven for 15 minutes until hot and lightly browned on top. These may be prepared ahead and kept in the refrigerator until needed (up to two days); add about an additional 20 minutes baking time if refrigerated.

Cafe Hash Browns

In a small town in Northern California, near Petaluma, there is one of those neighborhood cafes one finds across our country. These American treasures of atmosphere and good hearty morning food are a fine refuge from sterile chain restaurants, and a place where local neighbors go for a hot homemade breakfast and gossip over coffee refills. I ordered the cafe special: two fried eggs over-easy, bacon, toast, and hash browns. There are many concoctions that pass for hash browns, and it was an unexpected joy to find such perfect, crispy, splendid-tasting potatoes. I asked the young cook how they were prepared. He said the secret was cooking the potatoes ahead of time. This is an uncomplicated recipe and certainly very superior to premade or frozen packaged hash browns.

4 medium potatoes (white rose or red)
about 4 tablespoons bacon fat, vegetable oil, or butter for frying
salt and pepper to taste

Cook potatoes unpeeled in boiling water just until they are tender. Drain and set aside at least four hours, or preferably overnight, in a cool place (do not refrigerate). To prepare, peel potatoes and coarsely shred them, adding salt and pepper. Heat the fat in an iron frying pan. Make sure the pan is hot before adding potatoes or you will not have a crispy crust. Add potatoes and press down with a spatula. Cook 5 minutes, turn over, add a little more fat or oil if needed. Fry other side for an additional 5 minutes. Place hash browns on warmed plates. These potatoes make a fine simple dinner served with eggs and applesauce. This will serve 2–3.

Cobb Salad from Los Angeles

Cobb salad is the darling of Los Angeles restaurants. The salad was created by Robert Cobb, owner of the legendary Brown Derby restaurant. One evening, he arrived home after work very hungry and just made a big salad using the food in his refrigerator. It came out so well that the next day he re-created it at the restaurant. It was a hit there as well, and became a signature dish of the Brown Derby menu. Soon, other southern California restaurants were making their own versions, as movie stars and Hollywood executives went crazy over this attractive and delicious dish.

Cobb salad is a perfect dinner for warm summer evenings. Don't let the rather long list of ingredients intimidate you! After you've made the salad once, you will see how simple it is to prepare.

- ½ head iceberg lettuce
- ½ head curly endive (chicory) or escarole
- ½ bunch watercress
- 2 tablespoons minced green onion or chives
- 2 ripe tomatoes, diced
- 6 slices bacon, cooked crisp and crumbled
- 3 hard-boiled eggs, peeled and chopped
- 1 ripe avocado, peeled and diced
- 2 boneless chicken breasts, cooked
- 1 tablespoon fresh lemon juice
- 2 ounces Roquefort cheese (or other blue type), crumbled

Wash the lettuce and discard any bruised or "tired" leaves. Wash the watercress, removing top leaves and saving stems for another use (soup, etc.). Wrap the lettuce and cress in a damp towel. Place in a plastic bag and refrigerate to crisp (at least 30 minutes). Dice the chicken breasts and mix with lemon juice. Refrigerate.

To assemble the salad, cut the greens in thin strips and place in a large salad bowl or on a platter. Lay the diced chicken over the greens, followed by the green onions. Place the tomatoes on top of the green onions. Sprinkle the bacon in a strip along the right side of the chicken, and the eggs in a strip along the left. Place the avocado around the edges. Sprinkle the blue cheese where you think it might look attractive. Making this salad is a little like painting a picture.

Usually, French dressing is used on this salad. You can use bottled, or make your own by combining ½ cup salad oil, 3 tablespoons red wine vinegar, 2 tablespoons lemon juice, salt and pepper to taste, and a pinch of dry mustard.

Now, for the fun dramatic part. Bring the beautiful salad to the table and show it off. Then, right in front of your guests, pour the dressing all over it and mix all the pretty strips and things together in a big scramble, combining all the ingredients in the bowl. Serve at once to 4 or 5.

Hollywood Bowl Pasta Salad

Since 1922, the Hollywood Bowl has been *the* spot for music under the stars in Los Angeles. Summer concerts here feature the finest of music, and people from all over the world meet to picnic and then settle back for an evening of beautiful music. My husband and I have attended every year since we were married. We've taken our babies, and later our grandchildren, up to the top seats where there is room for little children to hear the music and then sleep. Other friends have joined us through the years to celebrate birthdays and reunions with a grand picnic before the concert, and this salad has always been a favorite on these occasions. It is versatile, as you can add pretty much whatever you want depending on what you're hungry for. It can be made ahead for convenience, which will allow the flavors to mellow. To make a complete meal of it, you need only bring some tasty bread, white wine, summer fruit, and cookies.

½	pound uncooked pasta—shells, penne, macaroni, etc.
3	tablespoons olive oil
2	tablespoons red or white vinegar
½	cup mayonnaise
	salt and pepper to taste
1	red or green bell pepper, chopped
2	green onions, minced
	options: chicken pieces, tuna chunks, slivered ham, peas, cold beef strips, bay shrimp, cheese cubes, olives, etc.
	Parmesan cheese and minced parsley for garnish

Cook the pasta per package directions, drain, and rinse with cold water. In a salad bowl, combine olive oil, vinegar, mayonnaise, salt, pepper, chopped bell pepper, and onions. Add pasta while still warm and mix all together. Add any optional ingredients you like; blend and refrigerate until serving time. Garnish with Parmesan cheese and parsley before serving to 4.

D.D.'s Ceres Carrot-Raisin Salad

Ceres is a small town in northcentral California, named for the Greek goddess of wheat, where my husband's best World War II Marine buddy and his wife Shirley moved after they retired. D.D. is the grand master of the local Masons, and of course we were invited to his grand inauguration dinner. The night of the dinner, we arrived to find D.D. in the kitchen supervising the salad preparation. The carrot and raisin salad to be served was his choice, a lifetime favorite for him as it is for many Americans.

4	large carrots
	salt and pepper to taste
½	cup raisins
1	tablespoon lemon juice
1	cup mayonnaise (or ½ cup mayo mixed with ½ cup sour cream)

Scrape skin from carrots and grate them coarsely into a bowl. Add salt, pepper, raisins, and lemon juice. Mix lightly. Add mayonnaise (or sour cream mixture) and mix. Chill for 30 minutes and serve to 4. Some carrot salad recipes use a cup of French dressing instead of mayonnaise; either way, it's delicious.

Snake Basin Idaho Applesauce

Applesauce is an American classic that has been served since colonial times as a side dish with meats and poultry. It is especially delicious with crisp roast pork, or as a simple dessert with a dollop of whipping cream. I am always amazed to see bottled and canned applesauce on store shelves, because applesauce is one of the simplest recipes to make. Freshly cooked, it has all the tantalizing flavors (and vitamins) of the apple. An added bonus is the wonderful scent of apples cooking that will fill your kitchen. Applesauce is especially popular in Idaho restaurants and cafes, as the apples grown in orchards along the Snake Basin are among the finest in the world.

> apples—any variety
> sugar to taste
> cinnamon

Peel and core the apples. Cut into sixths. Place in a pan with water just to the top of the apples. Cover and cook over a low flame until apples are tender, about 6 to 10 minutes depending upon the apples.

Stir, taste, and add sugar as desired. If cinnamon is desired, add a dash. Mash the mixture with a fork and cook an additional minute to blend seasonings. Sometimes a little horseradish is added to the sauce when it is to be served with meats. M.F.K. Fisher, the great American food writer, once told me that she liked stirring a pat of butter into her applesauce, and sometimes used brown sugar instead of white.

California Lemon Snow Bars

California grows most of the nation's lemons, which are harvested throughout the year. I once had the incredible experience of being a passenger in a tiny Cessna airplane on a low flight over a lemon orchard near Riverside. It was spring, and the scent of the blossoms drifted up to our plane. Below, the shiny citrus leaves with yellow lemons and pure white fluffy blossoms were beautiful to see. Lemon bars are made by first baking a buttery crust, then topping it with a tangy lemon mixture. Lastly it is dusted with powdered sugar "snow."

Crust

- 1 cup butter, at room temperature
- ½ cup powdered sugar
- 2 cups sifted flour
- ½ teaspoon salt

Topping

- 4 eggs
- 1½ cups sugar
- ¼ cup flour
- 1 teaspoon baking powder
- ½ cup lemon juice (juice of about 2 medium lemons)
- 2 teaspoons grated lemon rind
- ¼ teaspoon salt
- ¼ cup sifted powdered sugar for the "snow"

To make the crust, cream the butter and sugar together in a bowl. Sift the flour with the salt and blend into the butter mixture, mixing until smooth. Press lightly into a 13" x 9" x 2" baking pan. Bake in a 350° oven for 20 minutes.

To make the topping, combine all remaining ingredients except powdered sugar, and mix until smooth. Pour over the baked crust. Return to the oven and bake an additional 25 minutes. Cool in pan on rack. When cool, sift the powdered sugar "snow" over it. Cut into desired size bars. This recipe can be halved and baked in a 9" x 9" pan (the full recipe will make 3 dozen bars). They will keep in an airtight container for several days or in the refrigerator for a week.

Golden Gate Rum Pie

Rum was one of San Francisco's favorite drinks in the turbulent early days of the city. Rugged miners and sailors used their gold to buy intoxicating beverages, supporting 800 groggeries in the city by 1860. Today, fine wines have largely replaced hard liquors as the preferred social drink, but chocolate pie flavored with rum remains a popular and seductive favorite.

- 1 9-inch baked pie shell (a graham cracker crust is good for this pie*)
- 1 6-ounce package chocolate chips
- 3 eggs (2 separated)
- 3 tablespoons dark or light rum
- 1 pint whipping cream

Melt the chocolate chips in a double boiler or heavy pan over low flame. Cool slightly. Add one whole egg, plus 2 egg yolks and rum. Mix well with mixer at low speed. Beat remaining egg whites in a separate bowl with a mixer until stiff. Fold into the chocolate mixture.

Whip the cream until fairly stiff. Blend one cup of the whipped cream into the pie filling, reserving the remaining cup for the topping. Carefully spoon the filling into the pie shell and refrigerate at least 4 hours (overnight is better). To serve, spread the remaining cup of whipped cream over the pie. Garnish with a few chocolate curls or shavings. This will serve 6.

Drugstore Banana Split

When I went to Audubon Junior High School in southwest Los Angeles, my friends would gather after school and walk together to the nearby drugstore for some afternoon snacks. We were all hungry teenagers. This drugstore had a soda fountain with young men that served you. One of my girlfriends had a slight crush on John, one of the soda jerks. Joanne would flirt with him while he made our ice cream delights. I always ordered a banana split with a cherry Coke. Banana splits are still popular all over America, and are easy to prepare at home for a special dessert.

*For graham cracker crust, see "Key Lime Pie" in The South section.

1	ripe banana, peeled
1	scoop each vanilla, chocolate, and strawberry ice cream
4	tablespoons strawberry jam (or other flavors)
2	tablespoons chocolate sauce
2	tablespoons chopped walnuts, almonds, or pecans
	whipped cream
1	maraschino cherry

Split the banana in half lengthwise. Place the ice cream scoops in a row between the banana halves. With a spoon, dribble the jam over the ice cream. Top with chocolate sauce. Spoon the whipped cream over all. Garnish with the nuts and cherry. This will serve one happy person.

Classic Western Drinks

From its beginning, the West has had a reputation for drinking. Many have the impression from Hollywood movies that much of this imbibing was done by rough-and-ready cowboys sauntering up to rustic bars. Some of this may be true; however, there is also the heritage of the "rancho days." Fiestas went on for days because it was an arduous trip by horses or oxcarts over trails to reach the ranchos. Once there, it was feast and fun. Wine and brandy and various wine punches were offered to the guests. Traditionally, wine has always been offered with dinners in the West. Cocktails are popular in all the major cosmopolitan cities. Coffee is a favorite beverage, and today there are many flavored "gourmet" choices.

California is the wine center of America. The state's wines are famous worldwide and have won many international awards. It is not necessary to make a complicated ceremony of serving wine. White wine should be slightly chilled, and red should be at room temperature. Of course, there are numerous wine tests, tastings, and lofty adjectives used to describe the qualities of wine; however, the late M.F.K. Fisher summed it all up very well. She told me it is either a good red, or a good white!

California-style Martini

Cocktail historians mostly agree that the martini was invented in the late 1800s by a creative bartender in the small California town of Martinez. Martinis are having a new surge in popularity. As Frederic Henry (*A Farewell to Arms*) said, after two martinis, "I had never tasted anything so cool and clean. They make me feel civilized."

- 2 ounces gin
- dry vermouth to taste (usually a few drops)
- one green olive

Stir gin and vermouth together. Pour into a chilled 4-ounce martini glass. Add the olive. This will make one martini. Martinis should be made to order; do not attempt to mix ahead. Vodka is often subsituted for gin.

Irish Coffee

The Buena Vista is a bar and restaurant located at the corner of Hyde and Beach streets in San Francisco. This is where Irish coffee was first served in California. Stanton Delaplane, a travel writer, brought this recipe to the Buena Vista from Ireland's Shannon Airport. Irish coffee makes a very pleasant winter dessert.

- 1 jigger Irish whiskey (1¼ ounces)
- 2 sugar cubes
- strong hot coffee
- slightly sweetened whipping cream

Pour whiskey into a warmed glass. Add sugar cubes, followed by hot coffee. It is advisable to place a metal spoon in the glass to avoid possible breakage. Stir sugar and coffee together. I use a spoon to gently float the cream on top of the coffee. You do not want the cream to blend with the coffee, as the joy of an Irish coffee is to sip the coffee through the cool white cream. Use only real whipping cream. It should be whipped just until thick, but not stiff.

Orange Brunch Sangria

Brunch is a popular way of entertaining in the West. This orange-flavored sangria is the perfect beverage for brunch or summer afternoon refreshment.

    1½   cups fresh orange juice
    ½   cup sugar
    2   oranges, unpeeled, thinly sliced
    1   lime, unpeeled, thinly sliced
    1   red apple, diced, with skin left on for color
    ½   gallon dry white wine or dry red wine

Simmer the orange juice and sugar together for 5 minutes to make a light syrup. Cool, add oranges, lime, and apple. Add the wine and refrigerate for up to 24 hours.

To serve, fill a glass pitcher with ice. Add sangria. (If the weather is cold and wintry, the sangria may be served heated.) This will serve 8.

HAWAII

Mark Twain called the Hawaiian Islands "the loveliest fleet of islands that lie anchored in any ocean." It is true; these islands are like pearls spread out in the middle of the Pacific Ocean. Their volcanic land was thrust up from the depths of the sea in a series of violent bursts of molten lava which began 25 million years ago, and each of the islands has developed its own unique character and spectacular beauty.

Visitors usually come first to the island of Oahu, where they visit Honolulu. This is like no other city in the world, because people come here to celebrate! It might be birthdays, anniversaries, weddings, graduations, honeymoons, or other happy milestones. Because of this, the city is filled with a joyous vibrancy.

Honolulu is the first place I visited on the Islands, to celebrate a wedding anniversary with best friends who shared the same nuptial date. We went to all the sights: Waikiki Beach, Hanauma Bay, Pearl Harbor, the Honolulu Academy of Art, the Bishop Museum, and Waimea Falls. I was introduced to such island foods as poi, taro lomi lomi, malasadas laulau, and that unforgettable fresh papaya served with a dash of lime juice. Since that visit, we have returned many times and visited the other islands as well. I once wrote, and Gordon illustrated, a book about Honolulu cooking.

Kauai is the garden island. I have had picnic lunches with Hanalei friends, hiked in deep ancient valleys, and peeked in sacred caves. Once I saw a double rainbow over the sea. In Maui, I have felt the chilled winds that blow across the Halekala Crater. Once, with friends, we drove the curving Hana Road. At the road's end, we delighted in a Hawaiian lunch. There was a platter of sliced papaya and freshly baked coconut pie. We found and stood at the grave of Charles Lindbergh. On the golden sand beach at Wailea, my friend Ann and I placed our beach chairs in the ocean and let the little rippling waves splash over us. Neither of us wanted to return to the mainland, ever.

On the big island of Hawaii, I gazed at the red-hot molten lava, feeling as though I could see the goddess Pele watching over her volcanoes. This island is renowned for lavish culinary conventions in luxurious resort hotels, for multicolored sand beaches, vast ranches, sleepy towns, and authentic luaus.

The Hawaiian islanders are well aware of their precious food heritage. Farmers grow special foods to supply the increasing demand for fruits and vegetables from the Islands, while scientists and conservationists are hoping to bring a new awareness of the fragility of the plants and wildlife, many of which are to be found nowhere else on earth.

The dining in these islands offers romance in the tropical balmy air. Only here will you be served dinner garnished with orchids!

Island Rumaki

This Pacific-inspired appetizer, said to have originated with the Japanese population of Honolulu, is a favorite throughout the country. The flavors are tantalizing and it is fun to nibble rumaki from a little bamboo stick. It may be cooked over a low bed of charcoal, on a hibachi, or in your oven. The quantity of ingredients will depend on how many you plan to serve. For *each* rumaki, use:

- ½ strip of bacon
- ½ of a chicken liver
- ½ of a water chestnut
- 1 square (about 1" x 1") pineapple or papaya
- a sprinkling of soy sauce

Sprinkle the liver with soy sauce. Wrap the liver and water chestnut in the bacon strip, pinning securely in place with a large toothpick or a small bamboo skewer. Poke the end of the skewer through the pineapple piece. Place on a metal rack over a pan (to catch the drippings) in a 400° oven, until the bacon is crisp (about 15 minutes). If you use a hibachi, turn the skewer while cooking so each side is evenly cooked.

Portuguese Bean Soup

Portuguese bean soup came to the Islands with the first Portuguese immigrants, and is the most popular soup here. It seems everyone has his or her own version of the recipe. Local politicians, musicians, and schoolteachers swear by their family recipes, and often cook and sell their special bean soup for charity fundraisers. Beans, ham hocks, and cabbage combine to make a thick, tasty soup. One might call it the "minestrone of the Islands," because various ingredients of your choice may be added to or deleted from the basic recipe.

1		pound dried small red or kidney beans, or a combination of both
1		medium onion, sliced
2		ham hocks
		salt and pepper to taste
1		8-ounce can tomato sauce
2		stalks celery, sliced
2		medium potatoes, peeled and sliced
1		small cabbage, chopped or thinly sliced
½		cup uncooked small elbow macaroni
½		pound Portuguese or any hot sausage, thinly sliced
		watercress or parsley for garnish

Place beans in a soup pot and cover with 2 quarts of water (current studies have shown that it is not necessary to soak beans overnight). Add onion, ham hocks, salt, and pepper. Cover and simmer for 1 to 1½ hours, stirring now and then.

Remove cover and take out the ham hocks. Add tomato sauce and celery. Remove ham meat from bones, dice, and return to pot with remaining ingredients. Continue to cook for an additional 30 minutes. If the soup is too thick for your taste, thin with water or white wine. Garnish with minced parsley or watercress. This will serve 6–8.

Maui Onion Soup

The onions of Maui are very sweet and tender. Some island residents peel them and eat them raw like apples. Thinly sliced onion rings are added to salads and sandwiches, and are used for garnishes. An onion soup prepared with these special onions is especially delicious.

4	tablespoons butter
2	tablespoons peanut or sesame oil
6	medium Maui onions or other sweet onions, sliced thinly
	salt and pepper to taste
1	tablespoon flour
2	quarts chicken broth (may be homemade or canned)
1	cup dry white wine
	soy sauce for garnish

Heat butter and oil in a soup pot. Add sliced onions. Over a low flame, stir-fry until onions are limp but not brown. Cover and cook over low flame for 15 minutes, giving a stir now and then. Uncover. Stir in salt, pepper, and flour. Add broth and wine. Simmer over a low flame, uncovered, for 40 minutes.

This will serve 6. Add a few drops of soy sauce to each bowl for an island touch.

Baked Opakapaka in Orange Citrus Sauce

Opakapaka, a fish of the snapper family, is very abundant in Hawaiian waters and is one of the most popular entrées at Hawaiian diners. On the mainland, where opakapaka is hard to come by, you can make this dish with red snapper. Baking fish is a very easy and healthy way to prepare it. Hot steamed rice and chilled cucumber slices are the perfect accompaniment for this dish.

- 1 pound opakapaka (or red snapper) boneless fillets
- ¼ cup fresh orange juice
- 1 teaspoon grated orange rind
- 1 tablespoon soy sauce
- 1 tablespoon sesame oil
- 2 tablespoons minced green onion tops
- salt and pepper to taste
- orange slices for garnish (optional)

Combine all the ingredients except fish in a shallow baking dish large enough to fit all the fish in a single layer. Stir with fork to blend. Add fish and cover with marinade. Place in refrigerator to marinate for one hour.

Heat oven to 400°. Place the pan in the oven, uncovered, and bake 10–15 minutes or until fish is done. Baste fish with sauce once during baking. Be careful not to overcook. To serve, place the fish with sauce on two warmed plates. You may want to add a few thin orange slices for garnish. This dish is also delicious served cold for hot-weather dining. This will serve 2.

Hawaiian Pineapple-Beef Skewers

Cubes of refreshing pineapple, combined with marinated steak, make for a delightful dinner. This fusion of flavors is typical of Pacific cuisine. The basic recipe may be enlarged for an outside barbecue.

Last summer, while entertaining some friends from Switzerland, I prepared this recipe as a main dish. They complimented me all through the evening on my menu choice; it seems that beef is very expensive in their country and not often served. Pineapples from the Pacific are also difficult to find in Switzerland. These dear friends thought the dinner very exotic and tropical in a California backyard.

- 1 pound top sirloin or other tender steak
- ¼ cup soy sauce
- 2 tablespoons brown sugar
- 1 clove garlic, finely minced
- 1 tablespoon peanut or sesame oil
- 1 cup fresh pineapple, cut in cubes, or one can (8¼-ounce) cubes, drained

Cut the beef in bite-sized cubes (about ¾" x ¾"). Mix the remaining ingredients (except pineapple) and marinate the beef in them overnight, or for at least an hour. Remove meat, reserving marinade. Thread meat on skewers, alternating with pineapple cubes. Broil or barbecue until meat is of desired doneness, basting with reserved marinade while cooking. Serve with hot rice. This will serve 2.

Island-style Steak Teriyaki

It seems every menu in the Islands has some kind of teriyaki dish. It is a part of the culinary culture. The name comes from Japanese words: *teri* is charcoal and *yaki* is broil. There are many variations of the sauce. In Honolulu, fresh ginger and sugar are added to give extra zip and a little shiny glaze. This recipe can also be used with poultry or fish in place of the meat.

- 2 pounds top sirloin steak (or 2 pounds boneless fish or poultry)
- ¼ cup soy sauce
- 2 tablespoons sherry or sake
- 1 teaspoon crushed ginger
- 1 clove garlic, minced
- 2 tablespoons brown sugar
- 2 tablespoons sesame oil
- 1 teaspoon grated orange or tangerine peel (optional)
- lime slices for garnish, if desired

Mix the sauce ingredients together. Cut the steak into four serving pieces, place in a flat dish, and pour sauce over meat. Stir around so each piece is coated. Marinate at least 3 hours, or overnight if desired. The meat may also be cut in cubes and skewered.

To cook, remove meat from sauce, reserving sauce. Place under a broiler or over a charcoal fire. Cook to desired doneness, turning once. Dribble sauce over meat while cooking. This will serve 4. A few lime slices make an attractive garnish.

Polynesian-flavored Brisket

This beef brisket, with a blend of Polynesian flavors, is a real winner. I use this often for company, as it can all be prepared up to two days ahead, and guests always rave about this dish. Sometimes I double the recipe so I will have an extra brisket to slice cold for a picnic.

- 1 beef brisket (4–5 pounds)
- 1 cup soy sauce
- ½ cup dry sherry or white wine
- 1 cup orange, lemon, or pineapple juice
- 2 cloves garlic, peeled and minced
- salt and pepper to taste
- 2 tablespoons freshly grated ginger, or 1 tablespoon dried
- 1 cup fresh or canned pineapple, diced for garnish
- cilantro leaves for garnish (optional)

Place the brisket in a shallow pan or bowl. Mix together remaining ingredients except diced pineapple and cilantro, and pour over brisket. Make sure all parts of the meat are covered. Refrigerate at least 4 hours, preferably overnight.

Place brisket in a baking pan with marinade and cover tightly with a double layer of foil. Bake at 325° for 3 hours. Check during the baking to make sure there is enough liquid to keep the meat moist; if not, add extra soy sauce or fruit juice, being sure to replace foil tightly.

Slice meat, top with cilantro and crushed pineapple, and serve with warmed pan juices and hot steamed rice. This will serve 4 generously.

Diamond Head Sunset Papaya Salad

A Hawaiian sunset, viewed from Diamond Head, leaves a memory that is forever radiant. The end of day, fading into night over these Pacific islands, is always a dramatic sight. Once when we were visiting Honolulu, an exuberant member of our hotel staff recommended a dinner cruise. We quickly signed onto one for that very evening. The dinner and music were first-class, and the sunset was ravishing. The colors in this refreshing salad capture that mood in an edible way.

1½	cups red leaf or butter lettuce, washed
1	medium papaya, chilled
3	tablespoons peanut or salad oil
2	tablespoons rice vinegar
	salt and pepper to taste
½	cup salted peanuts or roasted macadamia nuts, coarsely chopped

Tear the lettuce into bite-sized pieces. Peel the papaya, remove the seeds, and cut into small cubes. In a small bowl, blend the oil, vinegar, salt, and pepper. Place the papaya and lettuce in a bowl. Pour on the dressing and gently mix. Sprinkle nuts over salad. Serve at once to 4.

Hanalei Bay Chicken Salad

Hanalei Bay is one of the treasures of Kauai. The beautiful curving bay, fringed with palm trees, is an ideal spot for picnics and a scene to remain in visitors' island memories. Our friends Marilyn and Ed moved there from Hermosa Beach many years ago. When we visited them recently, they had a picnic lunch all prepared. We sat on the warm sand by the bay and munched on this pleasant chicken salad. Marilyn had also brought freshly-baked banana bread, which was utterly perfect with our lunch.

- 2 cups cooked and diced chicken breast
- 1 8¼-ounce can pineapple chunks or 1 cup fresh pineapple chunks
- 1 cup trimmed celery, cut in small dice
- ¼ cup macadamia nuts or peanuts, coarsely chopped
- 1 teaspoon curry powder
- salt and pepper to taste
- ¼ cup mayonnaise or plain yogurt

Combine all the ingredients in a bowl. Mix together and refrigerate. This may be prepared a day ahead. Garnish with fresh cilantro leaves if desired. This salad will serve 4.

Pineapple Cornbread Muffins

When you are a tourist in Honolulu, it is fun to walk along the waterfront and to stop and have muffins and coffee at the various outdoor dining terraces. There is always a wide choice of muffins with island jams. Muffins, a legacy of missionary kitchens, have been improved with Hawaiian flavors. This one, combining pineapple and cornmeal, is one of the best.

- 1 cup flour
- ¼ cup sugar
- 3 teaspoons baking powder
- 1 teaspoon salt
- 1 cup cornmeal or bran
- ¼ cup shortening or butter, at room temperature
- 1 egg, beaten
- ½ cup milk
- 1 cup drained crushed pineapple, canned or fresh

Sift flour, sugar, baking powder, and salt together. Stir in cornmeal or bran. Blend in shortening with a fork or your fingertips to make a crumbly mixture. Add egg, milk, and pineapple, and stir to blend. Place in muffin cups or a well-greased muffin pan. Bake at 425° for 15 to 22 minutes, until golden brown. This will make about 2 dozen muffins.

Paradise Banana Bread

Most restaurants in the Islands serve baskets of fragrant, freshly baked breads with their meals. Banana bread is a favorite and is frequently served. As in this easy recipe, macadamia nuts are often added for local flavor.

- ⅓ cup butter or shortening, at room temperature
- ⅔ cup sugar
- 1 teaspoon grated orange or lemon rind
- 2 eggs
- 1¾ cups flour
- ¼ teaspoon baking soda
- ½ teaspoon salt
- 2 teaspoons baking powder
- 1 cup mashed bananas (about 2 medium)
- 1 tablespoon rum (optional)
- ½ cup chopped macadamias or walnuts

Cream shortening, sugar, and rind together. Add the eggs, one at a time, beating well after each addition. Sift the dry ingredients and add alternately with bananas and rum to make a smooth mixture. Fold in the nuts.

Pour the batter into a greased 9" x 5" x 3" loaf pan and bake at 350° for one hour, until golden brown.

Pineapple Upside-down Cake

Many people dream of a Hawaiian vacation. They imagine themselves swimming in balmy blue seas and sipping mai tais under a beach umbrella. Usually, pineapples figure in these reveries as well because the fruit has come to be so much a symbol of the state. A pineapple upside-down cake, with its tropical flavors, is a fine accompaniment for these daydreams. For best results, bake it in an iron frying pan!

- ½ cup butter
- 1 cup brown sugar
- 4 fresh or canned pineapple slices (reserve juice)
- 1 cup pecans or other nuts (halved macadamia nuts are good)
- 3 eggs, separated
- 1 cup sugar
- 5 tablespoons pineapple juice
- 1 cup flour
- 1 teaspoon baking powder
- 1 teaspoon grated fresh ginger (optional)

Melt butter over low flame in a 10½-inch iron skillet (or similar). Add the brown sugar. Stir to make an even coating in the pan. Remove from heat and arrange pineapple rings and nuts in the pan in an attractive design. A few maraschino cherries may be added to the pattern, if desired.

Beat the egg yolks, sugar, and pineapple juice together until thickish. Beat egg whites until stiff and set aside. Sift flour and baking powder; add to batter alternately with egg whites. Blend together until smooth. Carefully pour over the pineapple mixture so you do not disturb the design. Bake at 350° for 50 minutes. A wooden toothpick dipped in the cake center should come out clean. Loosen edges with a knife. Place a plate on top of frying pan (use pot holders) and turn "upside down." This cake is best served slightly warm. Sometimes it is served with a topping of whipped cream. It may also be baked in an 8" x 8" or 9" x 9" square pan, but the results with an iron frying pan are far superior.

Waikiki Coconut Cream Pie

The "star" of island desserts is coconut cream pie, a lovely mound of delectable coconut goodness that melts in your mouth. Any desired piecrust may be used; I like to use a basic graham cracker crust. Do remember, whatever crust you decide to use, not to add the filling too soon or the crust will be soggy. You only need enough time for chilling, so about two hours before serving is perfect.

- 1   9-inch piecrust, baked and cooled*
- ⅔   cup sugar
- 2   cups milk
- 3   tablespoons cornstarch
- 3   egg yolks, beaten
- 1   teaspoon vanilla
- 2   tablespoons butter
- 1   cup grated coconut (fresh is best)

Topping

- 1   cup whipping cream (8 ounces)
- 2   tablespoons sugar for whipped cream
- 5   tablespoons additional grated coconut for topping

In a one-quart saucepan, combine the sugar and milk. Heat over medium heat. Mix the cornstarch with the egg yolks. When the milk mixture is hot, remove about ¼ cup and blend with egg yolks. Stir until smooth, then add slowly to remaining milk mixture. Cook, stirring, over

---

*For basic piecrust recipe, see "Washington Apple Pie" in The Northwest and Alaska section. For a single crust, use one-half ingredient amounts. For graham cracker crust, see "Key Lime Pie" in The South section.

a low flame for 3 minutes. Remove from heat and add vanilla, butter, and coconut. Blend until butter is melted. Cool and gently pour into pie shell. Chill for about 2 hours.

Just before serving time, whip the cream with sugar until stiff. Carefully spread over pie and top with grated coconut. This will make 8 servings.

Cool Island Drinks

It is most pleasant to lounge on a shaded terrace in the Islands, sipping a cool tropical drink. These cocktails are often garnished with an orchid or some other exotic flower, and served with macadamia nuts. These are a few of the Islands' favorites.

Mike's Mai Tai

Mike Purpus is a world-famous surfer who has participated in many Hawaiian surfing competitions. This is Mike's original mai tai recipe.

- 1 jigger white rum
- 2 ounces orange juice
- 2 ounces pineapple juice
- 1½ ounces coconut syrup
- 1 jigger "151" strong dark rum
- ½ ounce cherry-flavored brandy
- splash of grenadine syrup

Mix white rum, juices, and coconut syrup together. Fill a 10- to 12-ounce tulip glass with crushed ice. Pour the rum/juice mixture over the ice. Add the jigger of "151" on top. Float the cherry-flavored brandy on top, with a splash of grenadine. This will make one drink.

Piña Colada

- 3 ounces white rum
- 3 tablespoons coconut milk
- 3 tablespoons crushed pineapple
- 2 cups crushed ice

Place all ingredients in a blender and blend at high speed until smooth. Garnish with a pineapple slice and serve with a straw.

Waikiki Frozen Pineapple Daiquiri

- 1½ ounces white rum
- ¼ cup pineapple chunks
- 1 tablespoon lime juice
- 1 cup crushed ice

Combine all ingredients in a blender and blend at low speed until smooth. Serve in a champagne glass.

Honolulu Sunset Cooler Punch

- 1 cup orange juice
- ½ cup lemon juice
- 1 cup pineapple juice, unsweetened
- 1 bottle (1 liter) ginger ale
- ice cubes
- mint sprigs for garnish

Combine all ingredients in a bowl. Garnish with a few mint sprigs. This will serve 4, however, the recipe may be doubled, tripled, etc. for larger groups.

INDEX

Alaska State Fair Barbecued Spareribs, 104
Alaskan Sourdough Starter, 107
All American Brownies, 97
All American Hamburger, The, 106
All Seasons Easy Cranberry Sauce, 24
Ambrosia, 74
America's Favorite: Hot Dogs, 152
Amish, 43
Anchorage Broiled Halibut With Olive-Cheese Topping, 103
Ann's Apple Cake, 45
Apple Pandowdy, 17
apples
   in Ann's cake, 45
   in German apple pancakes, 88
   in pandowdy, 17
   in Waldorf salad, 38
applesauce, 162
asparagus
   Polish, 89
   stir-fried, 156
bacon
   in Cobb salad, 159
   in Kentucky Scramble, 66
Baked Alaska, 111
Baked Opakapaka In Orange Citrus Sauce, 173
Baked Virginia Cheese Grits, 65
banana split, 164
bananas
   bread, 178
   Foster, 70
barbecue sauce, 37
bars
   coffee cinnamon chocolate chip, 114
   lemon snow, 162
bean soup, 171
beans
   baked, 11
   lima, 12
   red, with rice, 112

beef
   All-American hamburger, 106
   barbecued ribs, 104
   beer beef party stew, 82
   chicken-fried steak, 129
   in albondigas soup, 123
   in boiled dinner, 9
   in meat loaf, 149
   in Philly cheese steak sandwich, 30
   in red flannel hash, 10
   in Swedish meatballs, 86
   in tamale pie, 151
   in Texas chili, 128
   pineapple-beef skewers, 174
   Polynesian-flavored brisket, 175
   steaks with blue cheese topping, 105
   Swiss steak, 85
   teriyaki sauce, 174
beets
   in red flannel hash, 10
   Harvard, 13
biscuits, buttermilk, 92
Bloody Mary, 117
Blue Cheese Appetizer Dip, 105
blueberries
   in "slump and grunt," 18
   in spice bread, 13
Boston Baked Beans, 11
Boston Brown Bread, 14
Boston Clam Chowder, 4
Boston Cream Pie, 20
bourbon
   highball, 98
   mint julep, 75
   press, 99
   Sazerac, 75
Bourbon Highball, 98
Bourbon Press, 99
bread
   banana, 178
   blueberry spice, 13

Boston brown, 14
bread pudding, 69
Brennan's, 67, 70
Brennan's Bananas Foster, 70
broccoli
    in chicken Divan, 32
Brown Derby, 159
brownies, 97
Brunswick Stew, 60
cabbage, 9
Cafe Hash Browns, 158
Cajun Coffee, 76
cakes
    Ann's apple, 45
    baked Alaska, 111
    devil's food coffee, 94
    easy hot milk, 112
    sponge, 21
    pineapple upside-down, 179
    pumpkin cupcakes, 47
California Lemon Snow Bars, 162
California Mission Days Green Chili Rice, 155
California-style Martini, 166
Canyon Road Spicy Crunch Cookies, 133
Cape Cod Clam Pie, 7
Capitol Chicken Hash, 33
Cathy's Mom's Great Pork And Sauerkraut, 82
Celery Victor, 139
cheese
    in rinktum-tiddy, 10
cheesecake
    Chocolate, 41
    New York, 42
Chicago Polish Asparagus, 89
chicken
    cacciatore, 34
    Divan, 32
    hash, 33
    in Brunswick stew, 60
    in curry, 8
    in enchiladas, 148
    in gumbo, 58
    in tortilla soup, 122
    salad, 177
    Southern fried, 59
    Tetrazzini casserole, 148
Child, Julia, 83
chili, 128
Chili Sauce, 126
chocolate
    cheesecake, 41
    chip cookies, 23
    pie, 164
Chocolate Glaze Topping, 22

Chocolate Wafer Crust, 22
chowder
    clam, 4
    corn, 3
Cinnamon Toast, 93
clams
    in chowder, 4
    in Cioppino, 144
    in pie, 7
    in Utah casserole, 88
cob pie, 18
Cobb Salad From Los Angeles, 159
coffee
    Cajun, 76
    campfire, 117
    Irish, 166
Coffee Cinnamon Chocolate Chip Bars, 114
coleslaw, 39
Connecticut Strawberry/Rhubarb Pie, 19
cookies
    Canyon Road spice, 133
    chocolate chip, 23
    coffee cinnamon chocolate chip bars, 114
    peanut butter and jelly, 96
    Roosevelt sand tarts, 44
    snickerdoodles, 22
corn
    in succotash, 12
    muffins, 177
cornbread, 65
Corn Chowder, 3
crab
    deviled, 55
    in hot crab dip, 3
Cranberry Cape Codder, 25
cranberry sauce, 24
Cream Filling (for Boston cream pie), 21
cream gravy, 59, 130
curry, chicken, 8
D. D.'s Ceres Carrot-Raisin Salad, 161
Deli Double Chocolate Cheesecake, 41
Delilah's Utah Casserole, 87
Delta Queen Bread Pudding, 69
Diamond Head Sunset Papaya Salad, 176
Diner Greek Salad, 39
Don's Oyster Stew, 6
dressing, ranch, 132
drinks
    bloody mary, 117
    bourbon highball, 98
    bourbon press, 99
    cocoa, 16
    coffee, 76, 117, 166
    cranberry cape codder, 25

daiquiri, frozen pineapple, 182
egg nog, 48
gin rickey, 99
Irish coffee, 166
lemonade, 77
Manhattan, 49
margarita, 134
martini, 166
mai tai, 181
mint julep, 75
mulled cider, 25
piña colada, 182
Ramos gin fizz, 76
raspberry punch, 116
sangria, 135, 167
Sazerac, 75
sunset cooler punch, 182
tavern grog, 48
tea, 135
Tom Collins, 99
whiskey sour, 99
winter punch, 48
Drugstore Banana Split, 164
duck, roasted, 31
East Coast Steamed Lobster, 5
Easy Hollandaise Sauce, 33
eggs
    foo yung, 154
    in Kentucky Scramble, 66
    Sardou, 67
    spinach-filled hard boiled, 142
Eggs Foo Yung, 154
Eggs Sardou, 67
Ellis Island, 27
enchiladas
    cheese, 126
    shrimp, 216
Everyday Lunch Tuna Sandwiches, 155
Exotic Chicken Curry, 8
Farm Buttermilk Biscuits, 92
Feinstein, Dianne, 31
fish
    baked snapper, 173
    broiled halibut with olive-cheese topping, 103
    Catalina swordfish, 146
    Idaho trout, 145
    in cioppino, 144
    in Niçoise salad, 109
    tuna sandwiches, 155
Fisherman's Wharf Cioppino, 144
Fourth of July Macaroni and Cheese, 164
French Toast, 93
Georgia O'Keeffe Watercress Soup, 121

German Apple Pancakes, 88
Get-Well Milk Toast, 94
gin fizz, 76
Gin Rickey, 99
gingerbread, 15
Golden Gate Rum Pie, 164
Golden Glow Salad, 90
Graham Cracker Crust, 72
Granny's Ham And Potato Gratin For A Crowd, 83
Greenwich Village Chicken Cacciatore, 34
grits, 65
gumbo, 57
Halloween Pumpkin Cupcakes, 47
ham
    and potato gratin, 83
    in gumbo, 57
    in jambalaya, 56
Hanalei Bay Chicken Salad, 177
Harlem Barbecue Saudce, 37
Harvard Beets, 13
hash, red flannel, 10
Hawaai, 169
Hawaiian Pineapple-Beef Skewers, 174
Heartland, The, 79
hollandaise sauce, 33
Hollywood Bowl Pasta Salad, 160
Honolulu Sunset Cooler Punch, 182
Hoppin' John, 62
hot dogs, 152
ice cream
    in baked Alaska, 11
Idaho Rainbow Trout, 145
Illinois Lincoln Thanksgiving Pumpkin Pie, 95
Indian Pudding, 16
Indiana Devil's Food Coffee Cake, 94
Irish Coffee, 166
Island Rumaki, 171
Island-style Steak Teriyaki, 174
jambalaya, 56
Kansas Potato Salad, 91
kebabs, lamb (shashlik), 35
Kenai Campfire Coffee, 117
Kentucky Scramble, 66
Key Lime Pie, 71
lamb
    in shashlik, 35
Las Vegas Shrimp Cocktail, 141
lemonade, Southern, 77
Les Guthrie's Mother's Meat Loaf, 149
Lincoln, Abraham, 95
lobster, steamed, 5
Los Angeles Tamale Pie, 151

Luisa Tetrazzini's Chicken And Pasta Casserole, 148
macaroni and cheese, 64
Maine "Slump And Grunt," 18
Manhattan, 49
Margaritas, 134
Maryann's Jersey Tomato Salad, 40
Massachusetts Toll House Chocolate Chip Cookies, 23
Maui Onion Soup, 172
meat loaf, 149
Middle Atlantic, The, 27
Mike's Mai Tai, 181
Milwaukee Beer Beef Party Stew, 82
Minnesota Wild Rice With Mushrooms, 89
Mint Julep, 75
muffins
   jalapeño cheese, 130
    pineapple cornbread, 177
Mushroom Sage Dressing, 80
Mushrooms à la Russe, 29
Myrtle Grove Plantation Gumbo, 57
New England, 1
New England Boiled Dinner, 9
New England Drinks, 24
New Jersey Egg Nog, 49
New Mexico Albondigas Soup, 123
New York Cheesecake, 42
New York Cole Slaw, 39
New York Chicken Divan, 32
North Truro Blueberry Spice Bread, 13
Northwest and Alaska, The, 101
Orange Brunch Sangria, 167
oranges
   in ambrosia, 132
Oregon Blue Cheese Topping For Steaks, 105
Oregon Celebration Raspberry Punch, 116
oyster stew, 6
pancakes, German apple, 88
pancakes, sourdough blueberry, 108
Paradise Banana Bread, 178
Party Posole, 124
pasta salad, 160
Paula's Mystic Hot Crab Dip, 3
pears
   in Rio Hondo salad, 131
    poached, 115
Pelican Club Mashed Sweet Potatoes, 68
Pennsylvania Waffles, 37
Philadelphia Winter Punch, 48
Philly Cheese Steak Sandwich, 30
pies
   apple, 113
   Boston cream, 20

chocolate rum, 164
clam, 7
coconut cream, 180
key lime, 71
pumpkin, 95
pumpkin pecan, 72
San Antonio pecan, 113
shoo-fly, 43
strawberry/rhubarb, 19
Washington apple, 113
pieplant, 19
Piña Colada, 182
Pineapple Cornbread Muffins, 177
Pineapple Upside-down Cake, 179
Polynesian-flavored Brisket, 175
pork
   barbecued ribs, 104
   in baked beans, 11
   in meat loaf, 149
   in posole soup, 124
   in Swedish meatballs, 86
   in Texas chili, 128
   "pulled," 61
   roast, with sauerkraut, 82
Portuguese Bean Soup, 171
potatoes
   baked, 157
   gratin, with ham, 83
   hash browns, 158
   in potato salad, 91
   in red flannel hash, 10
   in watercress soup, 121
   Utah casserole, 87
pudding, Indian, 16
Pulled Pork Sandwiches, 61
pumpkin cupcakes, 47
Ramos Gin Fizz, 76
Rancho Days Fiesta Enchiladas, 147
Red Beans And Rice, 63
red flannel hash, 9, 10
rhubarb
   in pie, 19
rice
   in jambalaya, 56
   with green chiles, 155
Rinktum-Tiddy, 10
Rio Hondo Autumn Pear Salad, 131
Roasted Long Island Duck, 31
Rogue Valley Poached Pears, 115
rumaki, 171
Russian Tea Room, 29
Russian Tea Room Shashlik, 35
salads
   carrot-raisin, 161

Celery Victor, 139
Cobb, 159
golden glow, 90
Greek, 39
Jersey tomato, 40
Kansas potato salad, 91
Niçoise Northwest, 109
Waldorf, 38
San Antonio Pecan Pie, 133
San Antonio River Walk Enchiladas, 126
San Francisco, 144
San Francisco Stir-fried Asparagus, 156
San Pedro Marinated Vegetables, 140
Santa Fe Gazpacho, 121
Santa Fe Jalapeño Cheese Muffins, 130
sauerkraut, with roast pork, 82
sausage
   in gumbo, 58
Savannah Pumpkin Pecan Pie, 72
Sazerac, 75
Seattle Hot Cocoa, 116
Seattle Art Museum's Salade Niçoise Northwest, 109
Senate Bean Soup, 31
Shoo-Fly Pie, 43
shrimp
   in enchiladas, 127
   in gumbo, 58
   in jambalaya, 56
   in remoulade, 54
shrimp cocktail, 141
Shrimp Jambalaya, 56
Shrimp Remoulade, 54
Simmons, Amelia, 16
Skillet Corn Bread, 65
Snake Basin Idaho Applesauce, 162
Snickerdoodles, 22
Sonoma Spinach-filled Hard-boiled Eggs, 142
soup
   albondigas, 23
   bean, 31
   beer beef party stew, 82
   gazpacho, 121
   onion, 172
   peanut, 54
   posole, 124
   bean, 31
   tortilla, 122
   watercress, 121
   yellow squash, 142
Sourdough Blueberry Pancakes, 108
sourdough starter, 107

South, The, 51
Southern Fried Chicken with Cream Gravy, 59
Southern Summer Lemonade, 77
Southwest, The, 119
Stewart-Gordon, Faith, 29, 36
strawberries
   in pie, 19
Succotash, 12
Swedish Meatballs, 86
sweet potatoes, 68
Swiss Steak, 85
Taos Enchiladas, 125
tea
   iced, 135
Teddy Roosevelt's Christmas Sand Tarts, 44
Texas Chicken-fried Steak, 129
Texas Chili, 128
Texas Iced Tea, 135
Texas Ranch-style Dressing, 132
Thanksgiving Roast Turkey with Mushroom Sage Dressing, 80
Thomas Jefferson Deviled Crab, 55
toast
   cinnamon, 93
   French, 93
   milk, 94
Tom Collins, 99
tomatoes
   in gazpacho, 121
   in rinktum-tiddy, 10
   salad, 40
Tortilla Soup, 122
turkey, roast, 80
Turkey Gravy, 81
veal
   in Swedish meatballs, 86
vegetables, marinated, 140
Vermont Soft Gingerbread—1912, 15
Virginia Peanut Soup, 54
waffles, 37
Waikiki Coconut Cream Pie, 180
Waikiki Frozen Pineapple Daiquiri, 182
Waldorf Salad, 38
Washington Apple Pie, 113
watercress soup, 121
West, The, 136
Whiskey Sauce, 70
Whiskey Sour, 99
White Sangria, 135
Wichita Peanut Butter And Jelly Cookies, 96
Yellow Squash Soup With M.F.K. Fisher, 142
Zesty Catalina Swordfish, 146

MORE COOKBOOKS FOR YOUR COLLECTION

VINTAGE TEXAS
Cooking with Lone Star Wines
Frank R. Giordano, Jr.
Wine serving suggestions accompany each recipe, and wine is a featured ingredient in many of these 145 delicious recipes. Top Texas chefs, Texas winemakers, and other cooks contributed their talents to this imaginative collection of such dishes as Texas 10-15 Wine Soup and Country Baked Ham with Chardonnay Mustard Glaze.
1996. 220 pages, 7" x 10" jacketed hardcover.
ISBN 0-88415-856-X   #5856   **$24.95**

CONTEMPORARY MEXICAN COOKING
Anne Lindsay Greer
These tantalizing tastes range from unique interpretations of authentic dishes to new, imaginative cuisine created from classic Mexican ingredients. 27 masterful chefs reveal their favorite recipes.
September 1996. 240 pages, color photographs, index, 7" x 10" jacketed hardcover.
ISBN 0-87719-273-1   #9273   **$29.95**

THE HERB GARDEN COOKBOOK
Lucinda Hutson
> "This book is just lovely...The recipes sound delicious, brimming as they are with all those wonderful, fresh herbs."
> —*Bon Appetit*

230 pages, color throughout, photos, bibliography, source list, growing instructions, index, 7" x 10".
ISBN 0-87719-215-4 #9215 **$21.95** paperback
ISBN 0-87719-080-1 #9080 **$31.95** hardcover

THE CALIFORNIA COOKBOOK
Betty Evans
288 pages, illustrations, index, 8" x 8" hardcover.
ISBN 0-88415-197-2   #5197   **$21.95**

CUISINE OF THE AMERICAN SOUTHWEST
Second Edition

> "...Anne Lindsay Greer's sure sense of taste and clearly written recipes make this the best look available at one of our richest American cuisines."
> —**Richard Sax,** *Cuisine*

This award-winning cookbook presents delectable recipes, stunning full-color photos, menus, and how-to-do-it techniques.
292 big pages, full-color photos, illustrated section of ingredients, glossary with phonetic pronunciation, index, 8 ½" x 11" jacketed hardcover.
ISBN 0-88415-168-9   #5168   **$36.95**

THE ULTIMATE LOW-FAT MEXICAN COOKBOOK
Anne Lindsay Greer
Here's all the flavor and flair of Mexican cuisine, without all the fat.
144 pages, index, full-color photos throughout, 7" x 10" jacketed hardcover.
ISBN 0-87719-258-8   #9258   **$21.95**

Visit Your Favorite Bookstore!
Or order directly from:

 Gulf Publishing Company
P.O. Box 2608 • Dept. IW
Houston, Texas 77252-2608
713-520-4444 • FAX: 713-525-4647

Send payment plus $6.15 ($7.75 if the order is $30 or more, $8.65 for orders of $45 or more) shipping and handling or credit card information. CA, IL, PA, TX, and WA residents must add sales tax on books and shipping total. Or call with your credit card information. Or send your credit card information. Prices and availability subject to change without notice.

Thank you for your order!